Praise for
Rugged Individualism

"Davenport and Lloyd do an exquisite job in reminding us that 'rugged individualism' is and was a central feature of American character and civilization. More important, they detail the sustained attack on such individualism that commenced at the end of the nineteenth century, came to the forefront during the New Deal, and threatens to overwhelm us in the present. By focusing on the metaphor of 'rugged individualism' they have made a major contribution in the ongoing debate about American national identity."

—*Nicholas Capaldi*, *Legendre-Soule Distinguished Chair*
of Business Ethics, Loyola University New Orleans

"What is 'American rugged individualism'? In this short volume the authors not only answer that question but also provide a thumbnail historical sketch of its friends and opponents, a discussion of the ways in which it continues to shape our political debates, and a meditation on its future. Most importantly, they encourage the reader to engage these concerns and to come to their own conclusions on its importance and what its future should be."

—*Steven D. Ealy*, *senior fellow at Liberty Fund, Inc.,*
an Indianapolis–based educational foundation

In *Rugged Individualism: Dead Or Alive?*, David Davenport and Gordon Lloyd have produced a fascinating and insightful examination of a concept that is an essential part of the history and philosophy of the American spirit. This masterful analysis of a critical component of our national DNA, and the cogent exploration of its current status and future prospects, are most timely in view of our existing cultural confusion and moral ambiguity.

—*Ed Meese, III*, *former Attorney General of the United States*

RUGGED INDIVIDUALISM

Dead or Alive?

David Davenport & Gordon Lloyd

HOOVER INSTITUTION PRESS

Stanford University | *Stanford, California*

www.hoover.org

Hoover Institution Press Publication No. 676
Hoover Institution at Leland Stanford Junior University,
Stanford, California 94305-6003

First printing 2017
23 22 21 20 19 18 17   9 8 7 6 5 4 3 2 1

Manufactured in the United States of America

The paper used in this publication meets the minimum requirements of the American National Standard for Information Sciences—Permanence of Paper for Printed Library Materials, ANSI/NISO Z39.48-1992. ∞

Cataloging-in-Publication Data is available from the Library of Congress.
ISBN-13: 978-0-8179-2024-1 (cloth : alk. paper)
ISBN-13: 978-0-8179-2026-5 (epub)
ISBN-13: 978-0-8179-2027-2 (mobi)
ISBN-13: 978-0-8179-2028-9 (PDF)

CONTENTS

INTRODUCTION

B OTH AUTHORS have mothers in their late nineties. When one of us asks his mother about her favorite hometown sports teams, she says, "Oh, they're up and down, up and down." The other's mother likes to say, "Sometimes you win, sometimes you lose." Although we are more passionate and specific when we discuss our teams, there is something attractive about the greater patience and acceptance about the ups and downs that apparently come with older age.

American rugged individualism has had its share of ups and downs, wins and losses, since its birth at the founding of our nation and its coming of age on the frontier. We've sought to dramatize it a bit by asking in the title whether it is dead or alive. It's not a purely academic question since there have been those who have sought to kill it. As Henry Kissinger said, "Even a paranoid has some real enemies." Although it has taken some tough blows, somehow American individualism has lived to play another day. Indeed, we wonder whether the new social and business frontiers of the information age might be fruitful ground for yet another important chapter of rugged individualism.

Why should we care? Because rugged individualism is a unique component of America's DNA, a key ingredient in what makes America "exceptional." Underlying all the freedoms that the pioneers and founders sought to establish in the new country was individual liberty. It would be the individual, not the monarchy or the social class, who would be the essential unit of analysis and action in the New World. Herbert Hoover, who actually coined the phrase "rugged individualism" in 1928, contrasted it with the soft despotism and totalitarianism of Europe.

To place our work in the context of other writing about individualism, ours is not a book that looks at individualism primarily through the lens of psychology or sociology. Rather, we are interested in the political context in which American rugged individualism flourishes or declines. As Stephanie Walls argues in her 2015 book, *Individualism in the United States: A Transformation in American Political Thought*, at the founding American individualism was primarily political in nature, protected by the Constitution and fully compatible with democracy.

During the Progressive Era, however, rugged individualism became more about economics. Progressives both attacked rugged individualism directly and caricatured it as the myth of the robber barons and captains of industry. This economic critique of rugged individualism continues today through the work of French economist Thomas Piketty and others about income inequality, proposing both an economic and a political revolution in order to restore the equality of conditions that French journalist Alexis de Tocqueville found and admired in America.

Then, in the last thirty years, the battleground about rugged individualism has come to include the realm of sociology. Sociologists such as Robert Putnam and Robert Bellah worry that Americans have turned inward, staying home and disengaging from social and especially civic life. Putnam is concerned because Americans are now "bowling alone." Their solution is both a societal and a political transformation in civic engagement to protect against the dangers of rugged individualism, which they convey as anti-communitarian.

Our view is that, while nearly everything undergoes change over time, rarely is a transformation or revolution called for, especially over something as fundamental as American rugged individualism. Whereas the Progressives seek an economic revolution and the sociologists a social one, we see more continuity with the founding, believing that an awakening to the continuing value of political individualism is needed. Therefore, we go back in order to come back. We go back to the founding and to the American frontier in order to come back to public policy today.

As we travel the road of rugged individualism from the founding to today, we note persistent efforts to detour from that path, or even to destroy it. During the period 1890–1940, the Progressives launched full frontal attacks on rugged individualism and also sought to minimize and end its influence through caricatures of it as a myth of the rich. In particular, President Franklin Roosevelt's New Deal sought to replace the rugged individual with the forgotten man as the object of government policy. The rise of the New Left and also Lyndon Johnson's Great Society posed major threats to rugged individualism in the 1960s. Today, rugged individualism faces a host of enemies, from the rise of executive power, to the advance of narratives such as income inequality or our "antiquated Constitution," to the federal takeover of health care and education. But even rugged individualism's enemies acknowledge its continued existence.

We look with some optimism toward new frontiers of the twenty-first century that may nourish rugged individualism. There is a new "networked individualism" in the Internet age that is placing power back in the hands of the individual. Young people, through both their social media lives and their business careers, are making their own way as individuals on new frontiers. New books and popular television programs celebrate the rugged American spirit in conquering and overcoming new challenges. Although it is not clear how this might translate to the political realm, it could be that the very awakening to American rugged individualism we call for may already be in its early stages.

Perhaps as you read, it might help to think about where you stand on the matrix below (figure 1). Do you believe American rugged individualism is alive or dead? Whichever you find to be true, do you think that is good or bad? For example, President Barak Obama believes it is alive and well, yet he finds that to be wrong-headed and unfortunate. In the Progressive Era, historian Charles Beard thought rugged individualism was dead and that was a good development. Today Robert Putnam and Robert Bellah think it is alive and that it is a bad development for America. Your two authors think it is alive, if only barely, and want it to be strengthened. We place ourselves firmly in the upper right-hand quadrant. How about you? We trust you will find the resources in this book to help you better understand and appreciate rugged individualism.

David Davenport, Stanford, California
Gordon Lloyd, Malibu, California

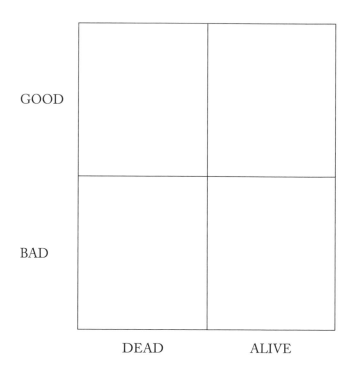

Figure 1: Rugged individualism matrix

Source: David Davenport and Gordon Lloyd

CHAPTER ONE

THE BIRTH OF AMERICAN RUGGED INDIVIDUALISM

RUGGED INDIVIDUALISM and American character are inextricably intertwined, the one essentially defining the other. Perhaps no expression better describes the uniqueness of America and its people than rugged individualism and a dictionary definition of that term would lead back to a study of American character.

When sociologist Seymour Martin Lipset sought to understand America, rugged individualism, accompanied by its first cousin American exceptionalism, was his path. "The emphasis in the American value system, in the American Creed," Lipset wrote, "has been on the individual."[1] Political scientist Louis Hartz searched for a unifying theme that would capture the essence of an American political philosophy. He, too, landed on individualism (and exceptionalism), calling "the reality of atomistic social freedom" the "master assumption of American political thought."[2] The economist F. A. Hayek argued that individualism was first a theory of society, then a set of political maxims, and the underlying basis for the economy.[3]

To be sure, individualism was planted deeply in the American soil in its founding era. The Declaration of Independence is thoroughly based in individual liberty; the Constitution, especially the Bill of Rights, is drafted in such a way as to protect it. The thinking of the founders, as revealed in the *Federalist Papers* and elsewhere, was fully grounded in American individualism. The American Revolution itself set the rugged tone of fighting for freedom. Truly something new and originally American was born in the founding period, something that came to be called American rugged individualism. As professor of religion C. Eric Mount Jr. has said, "Nothing is more American than individualism."[4]

Pre-American DNA of Individualism

Few things are created entirely from whole cloth, and antecedents to American rugged individualism should be acknowledged. Historically, the search for the roots of individualism would have traveled back to the Renaissance, when a spirit of discovery and creativity allowed individualism to flourish. In the last fifty years or so, however, historians have developed a case for the discovery of individualism much earlier, during the medieval era.[5]

Both the longest and oldest strand of DNA carrying principles of individualism into the American founding is religion, especially Christianity. The essential message of scripture, particularly in the New Testament, is the individual as a child of God, alone responsible to God for the way he lives his life. According to Jesus, God knows each individual sheep and calls them by name (John, chapter 10). The Apostle Paul pointed out that individuals receive different spiritual gifts (Romans 12:6–8) and, according to Jesus's parable of the talents, will be held accountable for their use (Luke 19:15). Free will and accountability, with individuals accepting God's gift of grace or not, are touchstones of biblical Christianity through the ages that provide a lasting basis for the individual as the basis of society. In the recent and valuable treatment *Inventing the Individual*, Larry Siedentop argues that the key to Western liberalism—individualism—has been strongly supported throughout the ages by Christianity.[6] The Protestant

Reformation reinforced—we would say reopened—the individual unmediated relationship between man and God.

Religious individualism was very much present and influential in the colonial period and the founding of the United States. More than 90 percent of the colonists identified themselves as Protestant Christians.[7] Another estimate holds that, at the time of independence, 98 percent or more of European Americans identified with Protestantism, primarily of the Reformed tradition.[8] Puritans and others of the Reformed theological tradition believed they, like the Israelites, were God's "chosen people," called to be a light unto the nations, a city set on a hill.[9] A study by Charles Hyneman and Donald Lutz of documents published between 1760 and 1805 reveals that quotations from the Bible dominated those from sources such as political philosophers Montesquieu, Locke, Blackstone, and others.[10] The book most often cited in their study was the Old Testament book of Mosaic law and history, Deuteronomy, which some found to be a model of civil government.[11] Sermons of the colonial and founding era citing "liberty" (Galatians 5:1), a "city on a hill" (Matthew 5:14), and other biblical phrases became a regular part of the conversation of that era.

As a consequence, the role of religion in the ideology and thought of the founding was strong and uniquely American. This was clearly acknowledged by the founders themselves. George Washington devoted a third of his first inaugural address to the role of providence in the founding, calling it "the invisible hand, which conducts the Affairs of men" so strongly in the United States.[12] John Adams acknowledged that the "general principles on which the fathers achieved independence were the general principles of Christianity."[13] Daniel Webster noted that Christian principles had become the foundation of civil society and said that "the Bible is a book . . . which teaches man his own individual responsibility."[14] This spirit of American individualism became part of the American mind through the colonists' and founders' devotion to Christianity and Protestantism.

At the same time, it is important to note the moderating influence of James Madison, Thomas Jefferson, and George Washington who, together, led a movement to disestablish and privatize the role of religion in America. During the colonial period, governmental regulation of, and reliance on, religious practices was considered a legitimate role of government. But once Madison and others laid down the principle of individual right of conscience, the role of government in the area of religious practices was reduced and confined. State constitutions and bills of rights in New Jersey, Pennsylvania, Delaware, and Virginia, for example, all recognized religious practice as a private right, not a matter for government support or interference. Privatizing religion made it a matter of personal consent, thereby increasing its character as a part of rugged individualism.

A second strand of DNA contributing to American rugged individualism was the philosophical individualism that came from Europe. Here the story becomes more complicated as different strains of European individualism led in various directions. The French *individualisme* carried a largely negative connotation. Jean-Jacques Rousseau attacked individualism—right along with private property, which he regarded as theft—in the eighteenth century, arguing that the general or collective will should predominate over that of any individual.[15] French philosopher and political economist Pierre Leroux, writing in the same general time frame, referred to individualism as laissez-faire and atomization, saying it produced "'everyone for himself, and . . . all for riches, nothing for the poor,' which atomized society and made men into 'rapacious wolves.'"[16] Meanwhile, in Germany the idea of individualism was more one of individuality, connoting unique characteristics or originality.[17] As Steven Lukes observed, the French notion was "negative, signifying individual isolation and social dissolution," whereas the "German sense is thus positive, signifying individual self-fulfillment and . . . the organic unity of individual and society."[18]

But of the European approaches to individualism, the work of John Locke and other Scottish Enlightenment political philosophers greatly influenced the American founding and its understanding and appreciation of individualism.[19] Writing in the seventeenth century, Locke identified the individual—not the class or the society or the state—as the central unit from which all analysis should begin. Everything else—class, customs, norms, rules, regulations—is acquired, Locke observed, so we should imagine the individual free of all those things and figure out what restraints enlightened individuals would consent to impose on themselves. Locke's reasoning was that the individual came first, with individuals then creating a society and ultimately a government, but only through the consent of the governed. Individuals are endowed with reason and freedom, underscoring that rights come before duties. A good summary of Locke's view might compare it to the Old Testament book of Genesis, though Locke would have said that in the beginning was the state of nature and that the Garden of Eden is a future garden of plenty if humans apply themselves and become productive.

According to Locke, the primary purpose of government, then, was to safeguard the natural rights of individuals. Governments were formed with the idea that the common good was a matter for public conversation and decision—the consent of the governed—not something preordained by the divine right of kings. Both political and religious arrangements, which had long dominated societies, were a matter of custom, Locke felt, and should give way to individual choices about them. Since government power was deemed to be a primary threat to natural rights, both natural law and social contract stressed protecting individuals from government power. Locke and those who followed in his classical liberal tradition tended to be suspicious about the search for the public good, as determined by some wise administrator or government official, and preferred individual liberty pursuing its own interests. One could summarize his view of the role of government as securing life, individual liberty, and private property, a phrase that would resonate and reverberate in the new nation's Declaration of Independence.

A third strand of DNA influential with the founders was economic, especially the work of Adam Smith, whose *Wealth of Nations* (1776) further developed John Locke's thinking about liberty, property, and individualism. In Book 1 of his work, Smith presented what he called "the System of Natural Liberty," in which he asked the reader to imagine what might happen to an economy if individuals were left to their own "natural" inclinations. In modern terms, Book 1 discusses how individual initiative, with a limited economic role for government, could increase the overall economic pie. He argued that the natural inclinations of individuals who grow and extend markets are more important in the story of human liberty and improvement than the planning and implementation of some centralized human wisdom. The free barter and exchange of individuals is a form of consent in a natural market system and is not planned. This sort of peaceful and productive state of nature allowed Smith to entertain an even more limited government than did Locke. Smith's notion of government is that it should be involved in defense, justice, and public works, the latter breaking down into facilitating commerce and educating youth.

Private property is the essence of this economic strand of individualism. In effect, goes the argument, God gave the world to man in common in the form of land. God intended that we should live well and gave us the means to do that. As rational and industrious people, we see the benefits of ruggedly working the land and, indeed, that also makes us happy. We privatize the land we work on, which makes us even happier because the land is ours. As we feed ourselves, the economy grows and we can trade our surplus. The right to own, then, what we have earned becomes a fundamental premise of American individualism.

The principles of individualism developed by these thinkers and others were not just a set of philosophical ideas but were believed to produce concrete benefits to a society that would follow them. Most practical was Adam Smith, who believed that individuals pursuing their own ideas and interests would create the wealth of a nation, what today we would call gross domestic product (GDP) or growing the economic pie. Only beggars, said Smith, rely on the benevolence of others for their daily bread. Free individuals were naturally inclined to "truck, barter and exchange" and thus participate in the project of improvement. John Stuart Mill, in his "On Liberty," would later elaborate on how individuals who are closest to the economic action will be more dedicated and innovative and will make better decisions than remote government officials. Locke believed that individuals who were free to pursue their own interests would be far happier and more productive. Indeed, when combined with the strong Protestant work ethic of colonial and revolutionary America, these ideas were especially powerful.

It is not surprising, then, that from these roots—Christianity and the political and economic philosophies of John Locke, Adam Smith, and the Scottish Enlightenment—would grow a spirit of individual liberty that permeated the American founding. It would be the intertwining and combining of these apparently diverse strands that would make American rugged individualism both so distinctive and so powerful. Thinkers from one dimension reinforced the contribution from the others. Private property, the core of economic individualism, is a necessary but not sufficient condition. Without the ability to make private decisions, the other forms of individualism are just misty dreams. Both political and economic individualism appreciate the importance of character and virtue that come from the religious strand. Adam Smith's "invisible hand" may be religious, we are not sure; George Washington's "invisible hand" most certainly was. So it was all three strands joining together that created American individualism. We agree with Yehoshua Arieli who said in his study of individualism in America that the term meant something very different from previous understandings: "self-determination, moral freedom, the rule of liberty, and the dignity of man."[20] These are the very themes one finds in the American founding, as America developed the notion of individualism into more than a philosophy of personal and societal life but rather into a political philosophy and system of governance. Americans exercise their rugged individualism when they consent to the government, church, and economy of their choosing.

The Founding: The Declaration of Independence

Long before the American frontier, which is popularly credited with the creation of American rugged individualism, came the settlers, the colonists, the revolutionaries, and the founders. In the rugged environment of new territory, they would begin to hammer out a philosophy of American individualism. As the writer G. K. Chesterton observed when he visited the United States: "America is the only nation in the world that is founded on a creed."[21] That creed, centered on individual liberty, would ring clearly from its founders and permeate its founding documents, the Declaration of Independence and the Constitution.

The Declaration documents a revolution, making a case to the "Supreme Judge of the world" for America's secession from England. From the first few sentences, the rationale developed by lead author Thomas Jefferson and others in the Declaration is England's failure to uphold individual rights, which are essentially the natural rights developed by John Locke and other Enlightenment philosophers. The very birth of the American republic, then, was defended on the basis of individualism. "We hold these truths to be self-evident," begins the second sentence of the Declaration, "that all men are created equal, that they are endowed by their Creator with certain unalienable Rights, that among these are Life, Liberty and the pursuit of Happiness." The document continues that "to secure these rights, Governments are instituted among Men, deriving their just powers from the consent of the governed," adding that "whenever any Form of Government becomes destructive of these ends, it is the Right of the People to alter or to abolish it, and to institute new Government, laying its foundation on such principles. . . ."

From the first words of the Declaration, the case for the new country was that the Creator had endowed individual men and women with certain natural rights and that securing those rights was the fundamental purpose of government. Since the king of England was abridging those rights, and other alternative means of redress having been exhausted, it was now appropriate to install a new form of government that would take these fundamental rights as their foundational principles. Indeed, by this way of thinking, individuals gave government its very power to exist, not vice versa. The era of republicanism had arrived in America.

Jefferson acknowledged his intellectual debt to John Locke, proclaiming Enlightenment thinkers Locke, Isaac Newton, and Francis Bacon "the greatest men that have ever lived without exception."[22] In a letter to Roger Weightman, Jefferson wrote that the "form we have substituted restores the free right to the unbounded exercise of reason and freedom of opinion. All eyes are opened, or opening, to the rights of man. . . . [T]he mass of mankind has not been born with saddles on their backs."[23] All at once, America was publicly committed to a Creator, to natural rights, and to a republican government whose purpose was the protection of individual rights and whose very creation depended on individual consent. This was revolutionary, indeed, since no nation had been formed on such a profound philosophical statement.

One way of understanding the significance of American individualism is that it was not merely a philosophy embraced by some people; in America, it was actually integrated into the founding and political framework of the new nation. For one thing, a failure to respect and protect individual rights was deemed a proper justification for first petitioning and then rejecting a government. Indeed, much of the body of the Declaration is a bill of particulars of the many ways in which the king of Great Britain had failed to protect and, indeed, had overrun individual rights, all of which were deemed a proper case for finding his governance illegitimate. Going forward from petition to rejection, the Declaration stated that "whenever any form of government becomes destructive of these ends, it is the right of the people to alter or abolish it." Protecting individual rights was the pass-fail level that a government must achieve or face the removal of the people's consent.

Beyond rejecting the king's leadership for a failure to protect individual rights, the founders planted American individualism itself deeply in the ground of the new republic. That which had been metaphysical and philosophical in Europe was now translated into real political terms. "Life, liberty and the pursuit of happiness" would become the fundamental rights and premises of the new nation. As Jefferson himself wrote in a letter to Henry Lee, in reference to the Declaration, "[I]t was intended to be an expression of the American mind, and to give to that expression the proper tone and spirit called for by the occasion."[24] American individualism would be the mind and soul of a new people and the foundational premise for its government, providing America's answer to Plato's question about what is the best regime.

The Founding: The Constitution and the *Federalist Papers*

It was one thing to declare that, unlike the king of England, government in America would vigorously defend individual rights and a government based on such rights. It was a further challenge, however, to develop and agree on the systems and processes of governance that would accomplish those goals. If the Declaration was the "why" of the American experiment, the Constitution, with all the debates leading to its adoption, would establish the "what" and "how." The Constitution would promise through its wording, and protect through the processes it designed, a nation based on individualism and natural rights.

The Bill of Rights, contained in the first ten amendments to the Constitution, is a remarkable statement of individual rights that government must not abridge but protect. The concept of positive declarations of rights had been part of Anglo-American legal history at least since the Magna Carta that, in 1215, proclaimed principles such as no taxation without representation and the right to due process of law. State constitutions predated the federal one, and most of them contained declarations of individual rights, many as the preamble to their constitutions. Although the form of positive declarations of rights had existed for centuries, the specific rights guaranteed by the states were frequently expansive, including not only legal process rights, such as trial by jury and due process, but substantive rights, such as bearing arms and the free exercise of religion.

As the founders worked toward a constitution, it seemed evident that with state constitutions protecting individual rights against state governments, a national constitution should similarly protect individual rights from a federal government. Although drafts of the document under discussion included limits on Congress regarding habeas corpus, ex post facto laws, bills of attainder, titles of nobility, and the privileges and immunities of citizens across the states, some delegates wanted more protections of individual rights from the government. Delegate George Mason proposed that a bill of rights be added, but it was deemed unnecessary. Later, following suggestions made by the states of Virginia and New York in the ratification process, the first Congress considered adding a bill of rights, with George Washington urging reverence toward "the characteristic rights of freemen" in his first inaugural address and James Madison declaring that he, too, was in favor of a bill of rights if everyone understood those were not all the rights Americans would enjoy.

At the end of the process, the first ten amendments to the Constitution had become America's Bill of Rights, declaring that individuals would enjoy freedom of religion and assembly, the right to bear arms, protection against unreasonable search and seizure, and so on. To satisfy Madison's concern that the Bill of Rights not be considered exhaustive, according to the Ninth Amendment, "The enumeration in the Constitution, of certain rights, shall not be construed to deny or disparage others retained by the people." The all-important Tenth Amendment added that "The powers not delegated to the United States by the Constitution, nor prohibited by it to the States, are reserved to the States respectively, or to the people." All of this is a part of the American DNA from colonial times, writing state and federal constitutions and consenting to legal documents.

But as important as these declarations of individual rights are, the processes in the Constitution that ensure protection of individuals from their government and from factions are equally important. Checks and balances, and separations of power among the branches and levels of government, were carefully constructed to limit government power over the individual. James Madison opened No. 10 of the *Federalist Papers* by pointing out that a "well constructed Union" allows the country "to break and control the violence of faction." Such factions, Madison recognized, are a "dangerous vice" that pose real danger to individual liberty and property when the "superior force of an interested and over-bearing majority" rises up. Rather than seek unrealistically to eliminate passions and factions, the founders saw that, in a large republic, one can pit the various passions, interests, and factions against one another so that the rights of citizens are not easily taken. Madison described this in *Federalist* No. 51 as "so contriving the interior structure of the government, as that its several constituent parts may, by their mutual relations, be the means of keeping each other in their proper places." To avoid too much power in the legislature, it would be divided into two branches; the overall government itself would be divided between two levels, state and federal; terms of office would be staggered and of different lengths; the president could veto legislation; vetoes could be overridden by a supermajority vote; and so on.

As noted in chapter 4, many of these checks and balances are under attack today as obstructing the work of government, but the founders had no doubt that they were important to protect individual liberty and property. Madison stated in *Federalist* No. 54 that "Government is instituted no less for protection of the property, than of the persons of individuals." Or, as founder Thomas Jefferson would put it a few years later in his first inaugural address as president: "Restrain men from injuring one another but leave them otherwise free to follow their own pursuits of industry and employment." American individualism had been not just the basis of a revolution against Britain but a political revolution in the founding of a new nation and political system.

Individualism Takes Root in the American Frontier

While America's leaders were planting individualism in its founding documents and governance processes, American individualism was taking root in the larger society of the new country. Indeed, rugged individualism is so closely identified with pioneering that it is often thought of as a creature of the American West. As James Bryce, British diplomat, historian, and ambassador to the United States, said in his important work, *The American Commonwealth*: "[A]n individualistic ethos, which began to emerge in American society during the late eighteenth century, became a dominant force—a fundamental organizing principle in explaining the ways that Americans have celebrated, justified, rationalized (and in some instances attacked) their social, political, and economic institutions along with their values, perceptions and beliefs."[25]

Several qualities about the American frontier contributed to the rise of rugged individualism. The very ruggedness of the land challenged the men and women who conquered and settled it to be rugged themselves. Forests, swamps, wilderness, mountains—all awaited these pioneers of early America. Traveling was a hardship; when one arrived at a settling point, there were mud huts and log cabins to be built. It is not surprising that America's heroes of this era were men like Davy Crockett, "king of the wild frontier," and Daniel Boone, who always sought more "elbow room." Theodore Roosevelt's *The Winning of the West* (1900) captures this "Pioneer Spirit" that produced a "rugged and stalwart democracy."

At a deeper psychological level, rugged individualism proved itself then, as now, an especially good match for frontiers. The sort of initiative required to set out to conquer new lands, territories, and ideas requires a certain rugged individualism. Then, too, the deeply religious nature of the American people contributed to the rise of rugged individualism. The pilgrims and Protestants, with their belief that they were individually responsible to read their Bibles and follow God as best they could, reinforced this individualistic mind and spirit. All of this contributed to an American mind-set that came later to be called rugged individualism.

The American historian Frederick Jackson Turner captured the powerful impact of the American frontier in his essays and papers, especially his famous "frontier thesis." Writing in the 1890s as an academic at the University of Wisconsin, Turner was the product of a frontier upbringing in rural Wisconsin, where he "mingled with pioneers . . . [and] from them he learned something of the free and easy democratic values prevailing among those who judged men by their own accomplishments rather than those of their ancestors."[26] Turner thought historians had it wrong when they claimed that Americans were simply transplanted Europeans whose environment had little to do with their spirit or character. Instead, Turner felt that the American frontier was decisive in developing the American mind and character. Indeed, the American character of rugged individualism also developed the American frontier.

In 1893, Turner delivered a paper on "The Significance of the American Frontier in American History" at the annual meeting of the American Historical Association. In it, he argued that key differences between Europeans and Americans had come about because of the physical environment in the New World, especially the availability of free land and the vast expanse of the continent that encouraged people to move ever westward. He continued the argument in "The Problem of the West" in 1896, noting that the "West, at bottom, is a form of society rather than area. It is the term applied to the region whose social conditions result from the application of older institutions and ideas to the transforming influence of free land." New land created "freedom of opportunity" for "new activities, new lines of growth, new institutions and new ideals."[27]

Turner, Alexis de Tocqueville, and others saw the American frontier and westward expansion as a great equalizer for American democracy. It "promoted equality among the Western settlers and reacted as a check on the aristocratic influences of the East," Turner said.[28] When land was widely available to people, both economic and political equality were readily available as well. Tocqueville put it more succinctly, calling the very "soil of America . . . opposed to territorial aristocracy."[29] Others would later argue those notions, noting that land speculators often stepped in, making free land a myth.[30] A crisis developed in the late nineteenth and early twentieth centuries when pioneers who reached the Pacific Ocean and the promise of westward expansion could no longer be part of the American psyche. Still, without question, the pioneering of the American West called forth rugged individualism, and Turner's explication of it was important in popularizing American rugged individualism.

It is also worth noting that accompanying the narrative of individualism in the American frontier were counter-narratives, or perhaps companion narratives, of community. The novelist and storyteller of the American West, Wallace Stegner, noted that "cooperation, not rugged individualism is the pattern that most characterizes and preserves it, spelling survival on the frontier."[31] Stegner points to collective action in "wagon trains, posses, barn-raising, communal harvests and quilting bees." Of course, individuals consenting to share rugged adventures with or near others does not undermine the essential nature of rugged individualism at work. We will nearly always find that American individualism is not naked individualism; it is accompanied by, or moderated by, something else, a theme to which we shall return in chapter 5.

Ironically, although Turner used the term "rugged" and also "individualism" in his work, he never put the two together—that was left for Herbert Hoover to do in a campaign speech in 1928. A further irony is that Turner is usually identified as a Progressive, a group that would later turn on and attack American rugged individualism as a mere myth and advance instead notions of collectivism. But Turner did not address that dilemma, lamenting later that "the frontier has gone, and with its going has closed the first period of American history."[32]

A French Philosopher Captures American Individualism

Among the most important observations about democracy and individualism were those made by a Frenchman, Alexis de Tocqueville, when he published *Democracy in America*. In 1831, Tocqueville and his longtime friend Gustave de Beaumont received a commission from the French government to study prisons in America. They stayed for nine months, with Tocqueville taking copious notes on democracy and individualism, not just prisons. Considering America to be a lens on the future, he wanted to record its opportunities and challenges in a new book chronicling a helpful analysis of the relationship between these two phenomena, democracy and individualism, at the founding.

By democracy Tocqueville meant a form of egalitarianism (equality of conditions) rather than a form of government. It is said that one of Tocqueville's discoveries in the new land was "individualism," a term that he is credited with defining and developing, if not coining.[33] Tocqueville called individualism "a recent expression arising from a new idea."[34] The word anglicizes the French *individualisme,* which to the French philosophers carried a negative meaning along the lines of selfishness, individual isolation, and self-absorption.[35] Tocqueville articulated the new idea of individualism as follows:

> Individualism is a reflective and peaceable sentiment that disposes each citizen to isolate himself from the mass of those like him and to withdraw to one side with his family and his friends, so that after having thus created a little society for his own use, he willingly abandons society at large to itself.[36]

One could say that Tocqueville saw American individualism as a mixed blessing: on one hand it created new freedoms and opportunities not available in aristocratic societies, but, on the other hand, it carried the risk that Americans would be so busy with their own affairs they would neglect the needs of the whole. As modern sociologist Robert Bellah concluded, Tocqueville "described [American individualism] with a mix of admiration and anxiety."[37] In fact, Bellah, Robert Putnam, Thomas Piketty, and other modern thinkers have concluded that American individualism has devolved into selfishness and believe that social equality is the solution.

While describing the new modern phenomenon of individualism in America, however, Tocqueville also saw other aspects of American character and society that would mitigate the dangers he saw in a selfish or isolating form of individualism. He noted how Americans were able to "combat individualism with free institutions" in an effort to allow democracy and individualism to work together.[38] Tocqueville was struck by the American inclination to use private associations to "give fetes, to found seminaries, to build inns, to raise churches, to distribute books," concluding that whereas "everywhere . . . you see the government of France and a great lord in England, count on it that you will perceive an association in the United States."[39]

In particular, Tocqueville saw something in the American character he called "self-interest rightly understood" that helped manage negative tendencies of naked or selfish individualism and moderate the inclination to abandon liberty in favor of equality. This practical quality of Americans to make "little sacrifices each day" for a greater good cannot really be called virtuous, Tocqueville thought, but nevertheless "forms a multitude of citizens who are regulated, temperate, moderate, farsighted, masters of themselves."[40] Even as the Constitution provided checks and balances on the government, American society had its own checks and balances against excess, even on individualism and democracy.

Notes

1. Seymour Martin Lipset, *American Exceptionalism: A Double-Edged Sword* (New York: W. W. Norton, 1996), 20.

2. Louis Hartz, *The Liberal Tradition in America* (New York: Harcourt, Brace, 1955), 62.

3. F. A. Hayek, *Individualism and Economic Order* (Chicago: University of Chicago Press, 1948), 6.

4. C. Eric Mount Jr., "American Individualism Reconsidered," *Review of Religious Research* 22, no. 4 (June 1981): 363.

5. See Walter Ullmann, *The Individual in Medieval Society* (Baltimore: Johns Hopkins University Press, 1965); Colin Morris, *The Discovery of the Individual, 1050–1200* (Toronto: University of Toronto Press, 1972); Aaron Gurevich, *The Origins of European Individualism* (Oxford: Blackwell, 1995); Larry Siedentop, *Inventing the Individual: The Origins of Western Liberalism* (Cambridge, MA: Harvard University Press, 2014).

6. Siedentop, *Inventing the Individual.*

7. Barry A. Kosmin and Seymour P. Lachman, *One Nation under God: Religion in Contemporary American Society* (New York: Harmony Books, 1993), 28–29.

8. Daniel D. Dreisbach, "A Peculiar People in 'God's American Israel,'" in *American Exceptionalism: The Origins, History, and Future of the Nation's Greatest Strength*, ed. Charles W. Dunn (Lanham, MD: Rowman and Littlefield, 2013), 60.

9. Ibid.

10. Charles S. Hyneman and Donald Lutz, eds., *American Political Writing during the Founding Era: 1760–1805* (Indianapolis: Liberty Fund, 1983), 191–92.

11. Ibid. We are aware of the debate surrounding this study's reference to sermons. On one hand, sermons were widely printed and circulated, perhaps outweighing their influence in the literature of the time. On the other hand, the study only included sermons that also cited secular sources, greatly reducing the number of sermons included in the study. The point is that scripture was very much in the air at the time of the founding.

12. Dreisbach, "A Peculiar People," 59.

13. In a letter from John Adams to Thomas Jefferson on June 28, 1813. Thomas Jefferson, *The Writings of Thomas Jefferson* (Washington, DC: Thomas Jefferson Memorial Association, 1904), 13: 292–94.

14. Daniel Webster, *Address Delivered at Bunker Hill, June 17, 1843, on the Completion of the Monument* (Boston: T. R. Marvin, 1843), 31; see also W. P. Strickland, *History of the American Bible Society from Its Organization to the Present Time* (New York: Harper and Brothers, 1849).

15. Jean-Jacques Rousseau, *The Social Contract and Discourses*, ed. G. D. H. Cole (New York: E. P. Dutton, 1913).

16. Steven Lukes, *Individualism* (New York: Harper and Row, 1973), 10.

17. Ibid., 17–18.

18. Ibid., 22.

19. John Locke, *Second Treatise of Government* (Chicago: BN Publishing, 2008). Others have identified Thomas Hobbes as originating the concept of the individual as the philosophical starting point. But according to Hobbes, the life of the individual in the state of nature was "solitary, poor, nasty, brutish and short." The only way for the individual to preserve himself, according to Hobbes, was to join a society in which government had virtual control over his life. So although Hobbes may have started out with the individual, he ended up with what we might call authoritarianism. We see Locke as a correction to Hobbes, standing for individualism in a positive light.

20. Ychoshua Arieli, *Individualism and Nationalism in American Ideology* (Cambridge, MA: Harvard University Press, 1964), 193.

21. G. K. Chesterton, *What I Saw in America* (New York: Dodd, Mead, 1922), 7.

22. Jefferson's letter to John Trumbull, February 15, 1789. Thomas Jefferson, *The Writings of Thomas Jefferson*, 939. We note Garry Wills's argument that Locke was not a major inspiration for Jefferson. See Gary Wills, *Inventing America: Jefferson's Declaration of Independence* (Garden City, NY: Doubleday, 1978), 229. But we believe the weight of the evidence favors Jefferson's reliance on Locke's work.

23. Thomas Jefferson's letter to Roger C. Weightman, June 24, 1826. *Thomas Jefferson: Writings*, ed. Merrill D. Peterson (New York: Library of America, 1984), 1516–17.

24. Ibid., 1500–1501.

25. James Bryce, *The American Commonwealth* (London: 1888), 2: 406–7.

26. Ray Allen Billington, "How the Frontier Shaped the American Character," *American Heritage* 9, no. 4 (April 1958): 4.

27. Frederick Jackson Turner, "The Problem of the West," *Atlantic Monthly*, September 1896, www.theatlantic.com/past/docs/issues/95sep/ets/turn.htm.

28. Ibid.

29. David M. Wrobel, *The End of American Exceptionalism: Frontier Anxiety from the Old West to the New Deal* (Lawrence: University Press of Kansas, 1993), 7.

30. Billington, "How the Frontier Shaped the American Character."

31. See Richard W. Slatta, "Making and Unmaking Myths of the American Frontier," *European Journal of American Culture* 29, no. 2 (2010): 84.

32. Frederick Jackson Turner, "The Significance of the Frontier in American History," *Proceedings of the State Historical Society of Wisconsin*, December 14, 1893, 112.

33. Alexis de Tocqueville, *Democracy in America*, ed. Harvey C. Mansfield and Delba Winthrop (Chicago: University of Chicago Press, 2000), 482.

34. Ibid.

35. Ibid., 182–83, 187.

36. Ibid., 482.

37. Ibid., 174.

38. Ibid., 487.

39. Ibid., 489.

40. Ibid., 502.

CHAPTER TWO

THE NEAR-DEATH EXPERIENCE OF RUGGED INDIVIDUALISM

FOLLOWING THE CIVIL WAR, Americans continued their westward expansion, especially when millions of acres of free land were made available in the late 1880s and early 1890s. These pioneers were classic rugged individuals, giving up home and family and enduring hardship to travel into unsettled territory. But during the period 1890–1940, rugged individualism fell on hard times. The closing of the American Western frontier, the shift from an agrarian to an industrial economy, the rise of Progressivism, and finally the New Deal all undermined American rugged individualism. By the time Charles Beard published his essay, "The Myth of Rugged American Individualism" in 1931, and Franklin Roosevelt's "forgotten man" seemingly replaced the rugged individual as the object of federal government policy beginning in 1933, one could reasonably wonder whether rugged individualism would survive.

The Closing Frontier, Industrialization, and Rise of Progressivism Undermine Rugged Individualism

If the American frontier was central to understanding and nurturing American rugged individualism, then the closing of the frontier raised serious questions about its future. For example, in their contemporary study, *Habits of the Heart: Individualism and Commitment in American Life*, Robert Bellah and his colleagues described the period of "rapid westward expansion and industrial growth" between the Civil War and World War I as "the most rapid and profound transformation" of American society in its history, bringing into being a "new national society . . . within whose structure we still live."[1] The decade of the 1890s alone was "a 'watershed' in American history," with huge population growth, including large-scale immigration and expansion of the industrial base.[2] The shift from a largely agrarian country always moving toward new frontiers to a more urban and industrialized society had a significant impact on national character, bringing the rugged individual under attack.

By 1890, the US Census Bureau officially declared that the frontier was closed and no longer would there be data tracking westward migration. Many social implications were thought to flow from this important demographic development. For one thing, the safety valve of moving west when conditions became too crowded or difficult was now gone. Americans would have to learn to live and work together under more crowded conditions. The United States would now be less "exceptional" and more like the busy urban centers of Europe. It was widely believed that American cowboys, pioneers, and rugged individuals had hit a wall—the Pacific Ocean—and that the country would never be the same.

Very quickly, the political and economic implications of the loss of the American frontier came to the fore, with a long-term debate framed by the following questions: If American rugged individualism was born of free open land and the frontiers of the West, did the loss of the frontier mean the inevitable death of rugged individualism? And, if so, what would take its place? The answers to these fundamental questions would reshape the understanding of American exceptionalism and individualism for the next one hundred years and, indeed, is one of the fundamental issues of our time.

One hopeful response was that rugged individualism would survive the loss of the frontier. It might be reshaped or reinvented, but it was too much a part of the fundamental American character to simply disappear from the scene altogether. No less a rugged individual than Theodore Roosevelt called for precisely this in his most famous work, *The Winning of the West.* Roosevelt, echoing the manliness referenced by James Madison in *Federalist* No. 14, argued that the pioneer spirit cultivated both a "vigorous manliness" that was essential to the nation and a "rugged and stalwart democracy" that had to be sustained.[3] As he boldly put it, "Unless we keep the barbarian virtues, gaining the civilized ones will be of little avail."[4] Kansas journalist and writer Charles Moreau Harger suggested that a "new Westerner" might emerge, combining some of the qualities of the old pioneer with some new ones. This new Westerner would be a "clear-headed, stout-hearted, frank-faced man of the plains; the product of years of trial, of experiment, of triumph."[5] In this way of thinking, American individualism might be maintained, with or without the ruggedness of the frontier.

But there were loud voices proclaiming that the death of rugged individualism was a natural and beneficial step in the development of the country. Robert Tudor Hill, in his 1910 contribution to Columbia University's *Studies in History, Economics and Public Law*, said that rugged individuals pursuing personal and family benefit allowed the wilderness to be conquered, but gave practically no thought to the increasingly important project of husbanding natural resources.[6] Later Harold Ickes, President Franklin Roosevelt's secretary of the interior, would be even clearer about this: "Denuded forests, floods, droughts, a disappearing water table, erosion, a less stable and equable climate, a vanishing wild life—these are some of the notable results of unchecked and ruthless exploitation by men who euphemistically refer to themselves as 'rugged individualists.'"[7] Roaming beyond his brief at Interior, Ickes added that rugged individualism in an economic sense "implies exploitation of the many by the few . . . and is founded upon the anti-social, unchristian theory of 'dog eat dog' 'may the devil take the hind-most.'"[8]

A growing conventional wisdom held that in the new, more urban environment of the country, the rugged individual would need to be replaced by someone or something else. This debate was every bit as varied and interesting as the ones over whether the rugged individual was gone or here to stay, or whether he was good or bad for the country. And it seemed that people of every political, economic, and professional stripe had something to say about it.

One common refrain was that, in an increasingly urban nation, America should turn toward a more European model of society and governance. The underlying theory was that, without the broad expanse of available land, Europe had been forced to develop institutional approaches—social, political, and economic—to the challenges of overcrowding that the United States now needed. Economist Richard T. Ely described the problems as maintaining a standard of living, along with poverty and class alienation, noting that it was a natural evolutionary step for a new nation to have to deal with "the normal conditions of human life" after the newness wears off.[9] In that sense, the loss of the frontier was a kind of reality check for America, and Europe offered experience and solutions.

Ely summarized the approach many believed should be taken when he said, "New economic and governmental directives were now needed to replace the frontier."[10] Historian Frederick Jackson Turner agreed that the nation would have to turn to "the realm of the spirit, to the domain of ideals and legislation" to preserve and develop the young democracy.[11] In today's language, more and different systems and structures were the answer and government should be the provider. This sort of broad commentary began to play out in debates of the day on issues such as land reform and immigration. Land reform, which had been focused on the fair distribution of cheap land, shifted its attention to how to utilize poorer land and how to conserve natural resources.[12] With concern over space, the immigration debate focused on new restrictions.[13]

It was in this context of shifting national priorities of the late nineteenth and early twentieth centuries that a new political force, Progressivism, rode to the rescue, or at least to the front of the parade. Unfortunately, its approach would emphasize aggressive government regulation and reform aimed at a more egalitarian society, all of which further undermined American rugged individualism. Indeed, a major Progressive piece from this era was a direct assault in 1931: "The Myth of Rugged American Individualism," by Charles Beard.[14]

One of the most influential Progressives, Herbert Croly, offered a case study of the movement's thought and its relationship to American rugged individualism. Later the editor of *The New Republic*, Croly wrote *The Promise of American Life* in 1909, a book that captured the essence of Progressive ideas. In it, Croly argued that Americans had lived in a bit of a dream state for the past one hundred years, one in which people could pursue their own individual economic interests without harming, and often even benefiting, the country. But now, he said, the "end of the harmony between economic individualism and national stability" created many "perplexities, confusions and dangers" for the twentieth century.[15]

In fact, Croly and the Progressives saw the seeds of this problem as having been planted in the founding itself. "Democracy as an idea was misunderstood" at the founding, Croly wrote.[16] It was the "meager, narrow" Jeffersonian ideal of "extreme individualism."[17] Worse, Jeffersonian individualism became attached to states' rights.[18] This "inadequate conception" of democracy and "feeble conception of American nationality" continued until the Civil War,[19] Croly said, apparently mocking Adam Smith's invisible hand, now that "automatic harmony of the individual and public interest, which is the essence of the democratic creed, has proved to be an illusion."[20]

In Croly's Progressive narrative, Americans were now awakening to the need for "constructive government reform."[21] Such reform would need to be national, rather than state or local, and most of all it would need to address the social problem: namely, the relation between capital and labor and the unequal distribution of wealth. To sum it up, "the government needs to be in the business of promoting 'social equality,'" Croly said.[22] There was an important educational component to this, in that the modern nation should teach "men how they must feel, what they must think, and what they must do, in order that they might live together amicably and profitably."[23] We needed a new Declaration of Independence based upon social justice, Croly thought, a new declaration of individual emancipation from the doctrine of economic individualism.[24] Croly and the Progressives felt that new conditions in America demanded both a new understanding of government and a new kind of citizen. The Progressive Party Platform of 1912, promising improvements to everything from country life and the workplace to health, conservation, and roads, along with aggressive government regulation of business, monopolies, and the like, illustrated the agenda of a post-individualism era.

What Progressives did to American rugged individualism was to first reduce it to a set of purely economic ideas and then to bash them by associating them with laissez-faire, devil-take-the-hindmost, selfish and wealthy capitalists. Never mind that American rugged individualism was a combination of religious, philosophical, political, and economic ideas. Progressives ignored the fact that Americans had founded a nation on individual liberty and consent of the governed, all part of rugged individualism. This nearly fatal attack on rugged individualism hit home because it reduced the argument to economic terms during the Great Depression, when economic concerns prevailed. But even the economic case for rugged individualism was not as simple and ugly as the Progressives portrayed it, nor was American rugged individualism a matter of pure economics.

Herbert Hoover's Defense of Rugged Individualism

Rugged individualism still had its defenders in the Progressive Era, notably Herbert Hoover, who was the first to use the term in a presidential campaign speech in 1928.[25] After observing that the "American system" was founded on "ordered liberty, freedom, and equal opportunity," Hoover pointed out that, during World War I, the country had necessarily federalized and centralized a good many powers. Following the war, Hoover argued that the country faced a choice between "the American system of rugged individualism and a European philosophy of diametrically opposed doctrines of paternalism and state socialism." Hoover's primary concern was that government not enter directly into commercial business itself. He understood the need for government to engage in public works such as "flood control, navigation, irrigation, scientific research, or national defense." And he was clear that he should not "be misinterpreted as believing that the United States is a free-for-all and devil-take-the-hindmost" society. He concluded: "The very essence of equality of opportunity and of American individualism is that there shall be no domination by any group. . . . It is no system of laissez faire."[26]

In fact, Hoover's thinking about rugged individualism predated his use of the actual term in 1928. In 1922, Hoover published a very thoughtful essay titled "American Individualism." It was widely admired, described by Fredrick Jackson Turner as containing "the New and Old Testament of the American gospel."[27] The *New York Times Book Review* said it was one of the "few great formulations of American political theory."[28]

To understand Hoover's thinking about American individualism, one must first appreciate his deep affection for the American system itself, contrasted with the systems of Europe where he had been working during the years before he wrote this essay. Soon after his graduation from Stanford University with a geology degree, Hoover worked as a mining engineer in Australia and China, and eventually all over the world. When

World War I broke out in London, he was asked to organize the evacuation of 120,000 Americans living in Europe, and he later organized the Committee for the Relief of Belgium. In 1917, he was asked to run the US Food Administration, helping feed America's European allies. After the war ended, he continued his food relief efforts in Europe.

When Hoover penned his "American Individualism" essay in 1922, he was in reaction against what he had observed in Europe. Indeed, he readily acknowledged that his faith in the American system was "confirmed and deepened by the searching experiences of seven years of service in the backwash and misery of war."[29] He saw Europe largely on a march to totalitarianism. In his Madison Square Garden campaign speech, he said that the European system "would extinguish equality of opportunity," adding that "for a hundred and fifty years liberalism has found its true spirit in the American system, not in the European system."[30] In the "American Individualism" essay, he underscored that he was not advocating "the individualism of other countries . . . but the individualism of America." In some ways, Hoover felt the zeal of an expatriate who had returned to his first love. As a starting point then, American individualism was decidedly not European and, indeed, stood as an alternative to the various "isms"— communism, socialism, syndicalism, autocracy, class—of Europe.

Importantly, Hoover distinguished American individualism from that of other countries in that American individualism "embraces these great ideals":

> [W]hile we build our society upon the attainment of the individual we shall safeguard to every individual an equality of opportunity to take that position in the community to which his intelligence, character, ability and ambition entitle him . . . we keep the social solution free from frozen strata of classes . . . we shall stimulate effort of each individual to achievement; through an enlarging sense of responsibility and understanding we shall assist him in this attainment . . . while he in turn must stand up to the emery wheel of competition.

Ours is not merely an individualism of contracts and law, Hoover wrote, but rather one resting on "philosophic, political, economic or spiritual grounds," each of which he elaborated at some length in the essay.

As if anticipating the Progressive critique of his ideas, Hoover was quick to point out in the essay that individualism needs to be tempered by something else, lest it "provide a long category of inequalities, of tyrannies, dominations and injustices." But he went on to point out that America has tempered its individualism "with that firm and fixed ideal . . . an equality of opportunity." The "sense of service" to others, Hoover said, is what "must soften [the] hardness" of American individualism. In that sense, Americans had "long since abandoned the laissez faire of the 18th Century—the notion that it is 'every man for himself and the devil take the hindmost.'" We abandoned all that, Hoover said, when "we adopted the ideal of equality of opportunity—the fair chance of Abraham Lincoln." We have gone even further in the twentieth century, he added, "with the embracement of the necessity of a greater and broader sense of service and responsibility to others as a part of individualism."

Hoover concluded his "American Individualism" essay by pointing out that individualism has been "the primary force of American civilization for three centuries," supplying all of her institutions. He argued that, rather than scrapping individualism in the industrial age, "What we need today is steady devotion to a better, brighter, broader individualism—an individualism that carries increasing responsibility and service to our fellows." Again, he emphasized the importance of individualism as the creative, social, economic, political, and spiritual force in America, tempered by equality of opportunity and service to others.

Historians strongly identify the expression "rugged individualism" with Herbert Hoover. After evidently coining the term in a 1928 presidential campaign speech, Hoover used it again in a pre-election radio address and several times in later years. In his 1934 book, *The Challenge to Liberty*, Hoover was overly modest when he said he "can make no claim for having introduced the term," acknowledging he "should be proud to have invented it."[31]

In a letter responding to questions from Princeton scholar William Starr Myers in 1938, Hoover wrote that his "impression is that the term . . . is an inheritance of Theodore Roosevelt's eulogies of American character."[32] American rugged individualism, Hoover continued in his letter to Myers, "aspires to equal opportunity [and is] regulated to prevent abuse and domination by others, as against the old European concept of *laissez faire*."[33] Hoover's historic understanding of the term and the underlying concept is well stated in *The Challenge to Liberty*:

> It has been used by American leaders for over a half-century in eulogy of those God-fearing men and women of honesty whose stamina and character and fearless assertion of rights led them to make their own way in life. It is they who have borne the burdens and given leadership in their communities. Rugged individualism is indeed a distinguishing and enduring quality ever found among Americans. It gives lifeblood to such basic principles as freedom of speech, conscience, press and equality before the law, regardless of race or religion. It contributes to the saving of our souls "from the deadening pressure of conformity and false ideals."[34]

This favorable notion of rugged individualism would hardly be recognized a few years later after Charles Beard, John Dewey, Franklin Roosevelt, and other Progressives had distorted and bashed it.

Economic Counterattack: Charles Beard's "Myth" of American Individualism and John Dewey's "Ragged Individualism"

President Obama must have been channeling his inner Charles Beard when he delivered his "you didn't build that" speech, pointing out how government infrastructure was essential to the success of Americans building businesses. Indeed, Beard, in his own essay (or polemic), "The Myth of

Rugged American Individualism," took on the question of just how rugged and individual were America's business successes of the day. Although the essay does not claim to be a response to Hoover, both the timing and language cause it to stand as a dramatic counterpoint to Hoover's own essay on "American Individualism" and his rugged individualism campaign speech of 1928.

Beard had earlier undertaken to expose the founders for pursuing their economic interests in drafting the Constitution.[35] Indeed, Beard's economic attack on individualism had, in a sense, begun there, essentially arguing that we should not view Americans as individuals but as members of a particular social class. In his "Myth" essay, Beard continued the Progressives' theme that so-called rugged individualism had been damaging to the country. As he put it: "The cold truth is that the individualist creed of everybody for himself and the devil take the hindmost is principally responsible for the distress in which Western Civilization finds itself." He admitted that it once may have been useful in the primitive days of American agriculture and industry, but now in a fully industrialized age it had "become a danger to society." Therefore, he concluded, "The task before us is not to furbish up an old slogan, but to get rid of it."

To this standard Progressive rhetorical assault on rugged individualism, Beard added a new dimension. He pointed out that a great deal of government's intrusion into the marketplace of business was actually at the invitation and even insistence of the so-called rugged individual businessman. Beard proceeded to catalog fifteen examples of government infrastructure projects and services that business sought or benefited from, including government regulation and subsidy of railroads, waterways, shipping, airways, canals, highways, tariffs (to hide behind), and departments (Commerce, Federal Trade Commission, et al.). Belying the "hands off" refrain from businessmen, Beard argued that under both Republican and Democrat administrations, businesses frequently sought supportive and helpful government intervention, creating a mere "myth" that rugged individualism was building the country.

In this same time period, another influential figure—philosopher and psychologist John Dewey—reinforced the Progressive agenda to move the country away from rugged individualism. In his 1930 book *Individualism Old and New*, Dewey argued that individualism was an economic battle for survival, noting that a kind of individualistic materialism ("ragged individualism") had crowded out equal opportunity, resulting in "inequalities and oppressions."[36] Joining Beard's attack on economic grounds, Dewey concluded that "the United States has steadily moved from an earlier pioneer individualism to a condition of dominant corporateness."[37] The corporation, rather than the individual, had become the unit of analysis as materialism came to the fore. In this new era, our problems were no longer from the physical wilderness but from the increasingly complex and important web of social conditions.[38]

Dewey was concerned about income inequality, noting that Marx was correct that all political questions "come back ultimately to problems connected with the distribution of income."[39] Dewey was alarmed that between 1921 and 1928 the number of millionaires in the United States had grown from sixty-seven to almost five hundred, twenty-four of whom had incomes over $10 million each.[40] Noting that "for anyone to call attention to this discrepancy is considered an aspersion on our rugged individualism and an attempt to stir up class feeling,"[41] he concluded that "we are in for some kind of socialism," whether public or capitalist.[42] So in the Roaring Twenties, we find concern about whether income inequality should prompt America to progress from rugged individualism to state socialism.

To solve these economic and social problems, Dewey turned to education, calling on schools to move away from cranking out students to run businesses and toward educating students to engage the "social problems of our civilization."[43] Indeed, it was Dewey's educational ideas that would become well known, urging Americans to turn their backs on the old "morals, religion, politics and industry," referring to them as "prescientific," and to integrate science and the interests of the community and society into the core of schooling.[44] The changing times meant that education itself needed to change, away from individualism, equated with selfish business and economic interests, to the larger needs of society as Dewey and his fellow Progressives saw them.

Herbert Hoover's Rugged Individualism
Confronts the Great Depression

It would have been interesting had there been a fair and sustained philosophical and political fight over the future of rugged individualism in the 1930s. But as history unfolded, the champion of American rugged individualism, Herbert Hoover, would be president when the greatest economic crisis of the nation's history struck. As noted previously, people were already calling for an increased role for the federal government with the closing of the frontier and the rise of the industrialized cities. But with the Great Depression leaving economic hardship everywhere in its wake, Franklin Roosevelt found a welcome reception for his ideas of government planning and action, all part of his New Deal.

Hoover's own philosophy of government is subject to differing interpretations. At one extreme is the perspective that Hoover was himself a Progressive who, as president, created New Deal-lite in an effort to stem the tide of the Depression.[45] On the other end of the spectrum is the conventional view that Hoover was a laissez-faire businessman who did too little in response to the Depression.[46] In fact, we have argued elsewhere that Hoover's philosophy of governance stood on two legs: constructive government and American individualism.[47]

Constructive government, an expression used by Hoover, was a set of ideas and practices about how the federal government should interact with the private sector in a time of postwar reconstruction and industrial and economic development. For example, it was Hoover's style, both as secretary of commerce in the Harding and Coolidge administrations and as president, to convene conferences of industry and government officials to communicate and solve problems, rather than turning first to government regulation as the solution. He saw government as an active catalyst, but not the designer, of solutions. Hoover was proud when he could carry out an initiative, as he did by limiting the work day to eight hours, for example, "without the aid of a single law" but by voluntary effort.[48] To Hoover, government could be vigorous but limited. As he noted in a 1928 campaign speech, the American system is unique, among other reasons because of a "new economic system" in which capital and labor work together "by joint effort."[49] All of this was combined with American individualism, as outlined in Hoover's 1922 essay.

Only months in office, however, Herbert Hoover's term was dominated by the Great Depression and became an emergency presidency. His theories about constructive government and American individualism were challenged by the need to provide help for millions of Americans thrown out of work and to manage the economic crisis. Hoover's core philosophy—constructive but limited government and individualism combined with equality of opportunity—prevented him from responding to the effects of the Depression in the dramatic way that Franklin Roosevelt would later do. Having solved worldwide food and relief crises with largely voluntary efforts, Hoover's initial instinct was to do so in the Depression, first calling business leaders to Washington to build confidence in the economy and urge them to keep up production and not lay off workers or cut their wages.

When the Depression seemed impervious to voluntary measures, Hoover asked Congress to save the major financial and economic institutions such as the banks, insurance companies, railroads, etc., which led to the passage of the Reconstruction Finance Corporation. He also rolled back tax hikes that had been put in place by his predecessor, Calvin Coolidge, hoping to stimulate the economy. He did not, by and large, spend federal money on direct relief to people, urging states, cities, and neighbors to do that. Part of his reluctance to spend money was his sense that a balanced budget was part of the formula to overcome the Depression. But his primary concern with greater federal government intervention into the economy was that such limitations on economic freedom in the short term risked burdens on political freedom in the long term. Hoover said in his acceptance speech at the 1932 Republican Convention, for example, that in all the "emergencies and crises," we must "preserve" the American system, which is "founded upon a conception of ordered freedom." He continued by saying that we should not turn to a state-controlled system that regiments men into tyranny, calling it our "first duty . . . to preserve unfettered that dominant American spirit which has produced our enterprise and individual character."[50]

In the end, some argue that Hoover's philosophy of rugged individualism and limited government prevented him from taking effective action to limit the Depression and its impact.[51] Others claim that Hoover engaged in too much government intervention, both laying the groundwork for the New Deal and potentially prolonging the Depression.[52] Still others point out that even Roosevelt's New Deal did not finally stop the Depression—that only occurred when America went on a war footing for the Second World War.[53] In any event, the Depression and its profound impact on the country provided an ideal climate for Franklin Roosevelt and his New Deal proposal to attack rugged individualism and to propose an alternative character as the object of federal policy: the forgotten man.

The New Deal Assault on Rugged Individualism

The 1932 presidential campaign became not just a contest between two men, Herbert Hoover and Franklin Roosevelt, but, as Hoover recognized, "a contest between two philosophies of government."[54] It was a clash between Hoover's continuing belief in the American system—individualism with equality of opportunity—and Roosevelt's proposal of an entirely "new deal" to shift power from individuals and markets to experts in the federal government. Rugged individualism was on the ballot, and in the throes of a worldwide depression, the people preferred government relief. As Harold Ickes, soon to become Roosevelt's secretary of the interior, put it: "In November of 1932 when the people were given a chance to decide at the polls whether or not they would continue the blessings of the individualism that by this time had become ragged, they repudiated in the most overwhelming vote ever recorded in a presidential campaign."[55]

In his campaign speeches, Franklin Roosevelt launched a brutal attack on rugged individualism while also laying out a comprehensive alternative. With unemployment at a staggering 23 percent in 1932, job creation became an obvious theme. We obviously could no longer count on the individual decisions of markets to create jobs, Roosevelt argued in a commencement address on May 22, 1932, at Oglethorpe University. Pointing out that the students who had entered college with the expectation of a job now had no job, he argued that happy times would not return without "the building of plans." The failure of the market, graduates were told, must give way to the egalitarianism and planning of the government.

In a striking parallel with public policy debates today in which companies at the forefront of the information age and technology have generated huge wealth, Roosevelt argued that the new industrial era of the 1920s and 1930s had likewise created wealthy titans at the top and income inequality. In the desperate times of the Great Depression, it was a message that resonated strongly. Roosevelt argued during the campaign that with bold, persistent government experimentation and planning, "we can bring about a wiser, more equitable distribution of national income."[56]

In another precursor of contemporary policy debates, Roosevelt accused the Republican leadership of a misplaced belief in what we now call "trickle-down economics." In his presidential nomination address at the Democratic National Convention on July 2, 1932, Roosevelt said that the Republicans were reactionaries who favored the few and hoped that their prosperity "will leak through" to labor and others. He pointed out that the economic rules of the market were not "sacred, inviolable, unchangeable" but "made by human beings." Roosevelt issued "a call to arms" for government economic planning and also for "bold leadership in distress relief." Roosevelt insisted that individual and market economic decisions were both inadequate and unfair and must be replaced by government intervention. In complete contrast to Hoover, Roosevelt made the contention that the American system itself was broken and in need of replacement.

Roosevelt's most powerful, comprehensive, and astonishing campaign address was to San Francisco's Commonwealth Club on September 23, 1932. He started by pointing out, "Democracy . . . is a quest, a never-ending seeking for better things, and . . . there are many roads to follow." His concern was that democracy was in crisis because America had entered a new age but was still holding on to outdated views. Bringing it all into focus, he said, "Clearly, all this calls for a re-appraisal of values. . . . The day of the great promoter" is over and the "day of enlightened administration has arrived." And the focus of all this effort must be on *everyman* rather than the individual. It is time, Roosevelt said, to recognize "the new terms of the old social contract." Once again, the times required more than temporary emergency measures, but rather the recognition that American individualism was over.

Remarkably, both Hoover and Roosevelt later gave speeches on two different anniversaries of the Constitution, Hoover's in 1935 and Roosevelt's in 1937, and these addresses illustrate their conflicting views of the Constitution and rugged individualism. Hoover's speech was a defense of the Bill of Rights, which he viewed as under assault by two years of the Roosevelt administration, noting that these were fundamental "rights of the individual in relation to government." Roosevelt, on the other hand, focused on the first three words of the Constitution, "we the people," noting that the people can do whatever they want with the Constitution since it is their document. Even on legal matters, Hoover's priority was to protect individual liberty and Roosevelt's was to use the system to enact changes to the American system in favor of the forgotten man.

Central Planning and the Forgotten Man
Replace the Rugged Individual

If American individualism had become a relic of the past, no longer appropriate for the times, what would replace it? Essentially two things, according to Roosevelt: (1) central planning and expert administration by the federal government should take the place of the series of individual profit-seeking decisions that brought on the economic crisis, and (2) the "forgotten man" should be substituted for the rugged individual as the object of policymaking.

Government planning was not Roosevelt's invention, but he was quick to appropriate and use it. As Yehoshua Arieli pointed out in his study of *Individualism and Nationalism in American Ideology*,[57] Progressives had struggled with how to replace individualism while maintaining "the peculiar pattern which distinguished the United States from other nations—its claim to represent a social order in which equality, liberty, and social justice were reconciled in the framework of a political structure."[58] To accomplish this, Arieli argues, the Progressives visualized "an immense enlargement of the functions of government in the service of social democracy" by which "it hoped to create a new center of loyalty and identification in the state."[59] According to commentators and historians of the time such as Stuart Chase, George Soule, and Charles Beard, the solution "was a carefully planned and regulated society."[60] As Secretary of the Interior Harold Ickes put it: "We have reached the end of the pioneering period of go ahead and take and we are in the age of planning for the best of everything for all."[61] Ickes laid out an even more comprehensive vision of how government planning should replace rugged individualism in his book *The New Democracy*:

> Wise and comprehensive planning on a national scale fits into the social vision of the future. If, as I believe, we are now definitely committed to the testing of new social values; if we have turned

our backs for all time on the dreadful implications in the expression "rugged individualism"; if we have firmly set our feet to tread a new and more desirable social path; if we have not given over the care and custody of ourselves and our children to the tender mercies of an outworn and ruthless social order; if it is our purposes to make industrialism serve humanity instead of laying ourselves as victims on the cruel altar of industrialism, then national planning will become a major governmental activity.[62]

Happily for the Progressives, they had already been at work on how experts might carry out central planning in government. In his work *The Study of Administration*, Woodrow Wilson argued that with the arrival of a more complex society came a greater role for government and the need for a science of administration. Rule by special interests in the society needed to be replaced by objective experts managing the administrative details through government. As against conservative mistrust of government and rule by special interests, the Progressives would rule by government experts and central planning. These complexities of government administration could no longer be handled by the public, who are like "a rustic handling delicate machinery."[63]

Franklin Roosevelt was quick to jump on the government planning bandwagon, both as a solution to the nation's immediate economic problems and as a long-term replacement for free markets and individualism. In a campaign speech on October 31, 1932, Roosevelt called for a "program of long-range planning." According to Harold Ickes, there were to be careful studies and planning about "commerce, industry and finance," including details such as navigation, flood control, power, sewage disposal, soil, climate, and crops.[64] In his Commonwealth Club speech, Roosevelt said everything must be reappraised: "The day of the great promoter or the financial Titan . . . is over. . . . The day of enlightened administration has come." Henry Wallace, who served as secretary of agriculture and later vice president under Roosevelt, said that there should be planning, but also "changing the rules of the game—with laws governing tariffs, money, the regulation of corporations, taxation, and railroad and public utility rates," all in the name of controlling "that part of our individualism which produces anarchy and widespread misery."[65] Robert Bellah and his colleagues, in their study of individualism, concluded, "The ideal of planning received a major push in the New Deal era when another, more collectively minded group of trained experts sought to repair the ravages of a corporate economy in disarray by creating a large national administrative state that would, for the first time, take responsibility for bringing a measure of order and compassion into economic life on a large scale."[66]

And the focus of all this planning was to be, not the rugged individual, but instead the "forgotten man." Ironically the expression itself originally meant something quite different from Roosevelt's version. A Yale professor, William Graham Sumner, coined the term to describe the man who pays for someone else's reforms that, in turn, benefit yet another person. Sounding more like Richard Nixon's later silent majority, Sumner said "the forgotten man . . . works, votes, generally he prays—but he always pays." But when Franklin Roosevelt used the term in a radio chat on April 7, 1932, he spoke of the poor who were left out by individualism and markets. He said, "These unhappy times call for the building of plans that rest upon the forgotten, the unorganized but the indispensable units of economic power for plans . . . that build from the bottom up and not from the top down, that put their faith once more in the forgotten man at the bottom of the economic pyramid." As *New York Times* columnist Timothy Egan would say seventy-six years later, with that radio talk in April 1932 lifting up the forgotten man, Roosevelt "found his theme, and the Democratic Party found its agenda for the next half-century"[67] (or longer, we would argue).

The Rugged Individual Meets the Forgotten Man

In many ways, two caricatures capture the central clash of the 1932 election: Hoover's rugged individual and Roosevelt's forgotten man. At one level, the outcome of this debate was heavily influenced by the fact that its first round was played out during the Great Depression. Importantly, however, Roosevelt was not satisfied to simply help the forgotten man with aid, but to undertake what he saw as needed long-term changes to alter the system in favor of the forgotten man. So he would say in his April 7, 1932, radio address introducing the forgotten man, that even spending billions of dollars to fund public works jobs for those out of work "would be only a stopgap." What was needed instead was a "real economic cure [that] must go to the killing of the bacteria in the system rather than to the treatment of external symptoms."

If not an unemployed worker who needed a job, who then was the forgotten man, and what did he need? He was a farmer, Roosevelt said in that same speech, whose purchasing power must be restored, without which "the wheels of railroads and of factories will not turn." The forgotten man was a farm owner or homeowner being dispossessed by the foreclosure of his mortgage, and the funds Congress and Hoover created for the big banks and corporations were not for him. According to Roosevelt, the forgotten man needed "permanent relief from the bottom up" rather than the temporary relief Hoover was offering "from the top down." The emergency demanded not relief but a permanent change in the system.

Roosevelt continued his attack on the rugged individual the next month in a speech at Oglethorpe University on May 22, 1932. The problem, he argued, is that "a society which values individual endeavor" results in a lot of "haphazardness . . . gigantic waste . . . superfluous duplication . . . dead-end trails . . . and waste of natural resources." We needed "bold, persistent experimentation," Roosevelt argued, to correct "the faults in our economic system" from which the forgotten man now suffers. He challenged the graduating class he was addressing not to make their way in the world, but to remake the world.

In his speech accepting the Democratic nomination on July 2, 1932, Roosevelt contended that the "consumer was forgotten." When the country had prospered economically in earlier times, the worker was forgotten and, in terms of dividends, even the stockholder was forgotten. Clearly the Republicans had some kind of amnesia! In this address, Roosevelt outlined in somewhat greater detail the kinds of economic planning and policies he would implement to protect all those forgotten men and women. "Throughout the nation," he said, "men and women, forgotten in the political philosophy of the government of the last years look to us here for guidance and for more equitable opportunity to share in the distribution of national wealth." In this speech he pledged a "new deal" for the American people.

In his sweeping address to the Commonwealth Club, Franklin Roosevelt expanded on the deeper principles behind the rugged individual–forgotten man debate. He traced it back to the clash in views between Thomas Jefferson, the champion of individual rights, and Alexander Hamilton, the advocate of more centralized government power. Once Jefferson defeated John Adams in the election of 1800, Roosevelt claimed, America entered a "new day, the day of the individual against the system, the day in which individualism was made the great watchword of American life." And, according to Roosevelt's narrative, the Western frontier with its free land made that day economically fruitful, long, and splendid. But with the Industrial Revolution things began to change and government needed to change with it. Roosevelt stated flat out, and in direct contradiction to Herbert Hoover's core philosophy, "[E]quality of opportunity as we have known it no longer exists." Roosevelt said "every man" has a right to his own property and the safety of his savings. So the forgotten man was now *everyman*.

Meanwhile, Hoover argued in the campaign that government should strengthen and support crucial systems but should also "preserve the fundamental principles of our social and economic system," which Roosevelt clearly intended to change.[68] The system, Hoover said, was based on "ordered freedom" and "equality of opportunity to every individual." Hoover's rugged individual was not permitted to "run riot in selfishness or to over-ride equality of opportunity for others." We don't need "haphazard experimentation" or "revolution," Hoover added. The government must help lead the way through the economic crisis, Hoover acknowledged, but "our first duty is to preserve unfettered that dominant American spirit which has produced our enterprise and individual character."

The election of 1932 provided a decisive answer to this debate in favor of the forgotten man. This outcome was understood by many to be a death blow for the American rugged individual. A column in the *New York Times Magazine* in March 1934 addressed those "who profess the greatest fear lest the New Deal may destroy our rugged individualism."[69] New York University professor Henry Steele Commager used the title "Farewell to Laissez-Faire" for his article in *Current History* in August 1933.

The Political, Economic, and Spiritual Assault on Rugged Individualism

Looking back on the Progressive Era and the New Deal, it is evident that a comprehensive assault was mounted against rugged individualism using political, economic, and spiritual weapons. The political attack was led by Woodrow Wilson and his effort to replace political decision-making with the expertise of the enlightened administrator. The attack became more direct when Progressives began to distort the real meaning of rugged individualism—individual liberty—with the economic argument that it was merely a disguise for robber barons and laissez-faire capitalism. Then, finally, it was left to Franklin Roosevelt to build the spiritual and philosophical case against rugged individualism with his plea that equality of opportunity was dead in America and government needed to systematically identify, plan, and meet the needs of the forgotten man.

Changes in the American political system that ultimately harmed rugged individualism were advanced by Woodrow Wilson in a series of books on government, including *Cabinet Government* (1879), *Congressional Government* (1885), *The Study of Public Administration* (1886), and *Constitutional Government* (1908). The heart of the matter was developed in *The Study of Public Administration*, where Wilson made the case that a merit-oriented administration should be separated from the spoils system of politics. Wilson argued that administrative questions were not political matters and should be handled by experts. With the arrival of a more complex society, there should be a new science of public administration, as had been developed in Europe.

Of course, these government and political reforms were not neutral. Their aim was to grow the small government from its Jeffersonian roots into a larger and more robust check on individual and corporate interests. As John Halpin and Conor P. Williams put it in a report from the Center for American Progress: "Progressives believed that formal legal freedom alone—the negative protections against government intrusions on personal liberty—were not enough to provide the effective freedom necessary . . . in an age of rising inequality, paltry wages, and labor abuses."[70] It was left to Franklin Roosevelt to implement these political changes with the central planning of the New Deal. Indeed, a refrain of New Dealers was that they were not just fixing the short-term problems of the Depression, but fundamentally altering the system in such a way as to prevent future such problems. Their aim was to "change the American political economy forever."[71] This was enabled by the rise of administrative experts with their alphabet soup agencies and the development of central government planning (which Herbert Hoover called "economic regimentation") of the economy, all of which diminished the place of rugged individualism.

The greatest challenge to rugged individualism in this era was its distortion from a term expressing individual liberty in a broad philosophical and political sense to a label for robber barons and the laissez-faire economy. "Laissez faire," from the French, means to leave alone or allow to do. Over the centuries, it had come to mean that government does certain central and indispensable things, while individuals and markets were left alone or free to do other things. Even John Maynard Keynes, for example, agreed with Edmund Burke when he termed "one of the finest problems in legislation, namely, to determine what the State ought to take upon itself to direct by the public wisdom, and what it ought to leave, with as little interference as possible, to individual exertion."[72] John Stuart Mill, in his *Principles of Political Economy*, favored "restricting to the narrowest compass the intervention of a public authority in the business of the community," saying such "laissez-faire . . . should be the general practice; every departure from it, unless required by some great good, is a certain evil."[73]

Early thinkers about what came to be the American understanding of laissez faire, the Physiocrats and Adam Smith, would limit government activity to "the enforcement of peace and of 'justice' in the restricted sense of commutative justice, to defense against foreign enemies, and to public works regarded as essential and as impossible or highly improbable of establishment by private enterprise."[74] Beyond these essential functions, and especially in the marketplace, people and enterprises were left to operate freely. Friedrich Hayek, in his *Road to Serfdom*, would point out that even in the economic realm, everyone agreed on planned or "consciously directed" activity—the question was whether such planning must be done centrally by a regulator or left to markets, individuals, and firms. The latter, he continued, was not an argument for "laissez faire" or "leaving things just as they are," but rather an argument for allowing those closest to the action and directly involved in the competition to "coordinate human efforts."[75] So rugged individualism was not simply laissez-faire economics; it was a matter of individual freedom which, even in the economic sphere, meant protecting, to the extent possible, individual freedom, not giving in to unnecessary government regulation.

But the Progressives largely succeeded in undermining rugged individualism rhetorically by portraying it as synonymous with laissez-faire economics. For example, Walter Weyl, one of the intellectual leaders of the Progressive movement, wrote: "The self-reliant, aggressive, individualism of the pioneer was also the spirit of the American factory builder, town boomer, railroad wrecker, promoter, trust manipulator, and a long line of spectacularly successful industrial leaders."[76] Harold Ickes, in his book *The New Democracy*, said rugged individualism had been characterized by "the acquisitive, exploiting, lawless qualities of a ruthless minority who would achieve wealth and power regardless of the rights of others," adding that it "implies exploitation of the many by the few."[77] In his essay "Farewell to Laissez-Faire," liberal spokesman and historian Henry Steele Commager said that the first hundred days of Roosevelt's administration had marked a healthy "repudiation of obsolete shibboleths of individualism and laissez-faire and a full throated assertion of the right and purpose of democratic society to readjust its legal machinery to the demands of a new order."[78]

Herbert Hoover argued vigorously that rugged individualism was "no system of laissez faire." Nor, he added, was it "free-for-all and devil-take-the-hindmost."[79] To the contrary, Hoover pointed out, rugged individualism in America was conditioned by equality of opportunity, not subject to the class systems of Europe. Still, under the pressure of the Great Depression, his message was not always heard clearly. In the end, the combination of Progressive rhetoric and New Deal action marginalized rugged individualism as a relic of America's past and sought to limit and replace it with government planning of the economy and the New Deal's focus on the forgotten man.

This Progressive challenge would be the first of several near-death experiences for America's rugged individual who, somehow, managed to survive. There would later be new frontiers, calling for a revival of rugged individualism. New calls for individual liberty would go forth in the land. Progressivism and the New Deal were not the last word. To paraphrase Mark Twain, reports of the death of rugged individualism turned out to be exaggerated.

Notes

1. Robert N. Bellah, Richard Madsen, William M. Sullivan, Ann Swidler, and Steven M. Tipton, *Habits of the Heart: Individualism and Commitment in American Life* (Berkeley, CA: University of California Press, 2008), 42.

2. David M. Wrobel, *The End of American Exceptionalism: Frontier Anxiety from the Old West to the New Deal* (Lawrence, KS: University Press of Kansas, 1993), 42–50.

3. Ibid., 66.

4. Ibid.

5. Ibid., 93.

6. Robert Tudor Hill, "The Public Domain and Democracy: A Study of Social, Economic and Political Problems in the United States in Relation to Western Development," in *Studies in History, Economics and Public Law*, vol. 38, ed. Political Science Faculty of Columbia University (New York: Columbia University Press, 1910), 217.

7. Harold L. Ickes, *The New Democracy* (New York: W. W. Norton, 1934), 19.

8. Ibid., 32.

9. Wrobel, *End of American Exceptionalism*, 38.

10. Ibid., 74.

11. Ibid., 78.

12. Ibid., 42–43.

13. Ibid., 47–49.

14. Charles A. Beard, "The Myth of Rugged American Individualism," *Harper's Monthly Magazine*, December 1931, 13.

15. David W. Levy, *Herbert Croly of* The New Republic: *The Life and Thought of an American Progressive* (Princeton, NJ: Princeton University Press, 1985), 97.

16. Herbert David Croly, *The Promise of American Life* (1909; repr., New York: BiblioBazaar, 2006), 42.

17. Ibid., 51.

18. Ibid., 59.

19. Ibid., 60.

20. Ibid., 152.

21. Ibid., 100.

22. Ibid., 195.

23. Ibid., 284.

24. Ibid., 266–72, 415, 421.

25. The term "rugged individualism" did appear in a newspaper headline about a speech by President Warren G. Harding in Meacham, Oregon on July 3, 1923. It does not appear that Harding himself used the term in his address, but a subhead in an article about the speech in the *New York Times* said: "He pleads for rugged individualism of the pioneers as against paternalism." Still, we believe Hoover was the first official or writer to use the term in a substantive way. *New York Times*, "Harding Takes Part in Pioneer Pageant of the Oregon Trail," July 4, 1923, 1.

26. Gordon Lloyd, *The Two Faces of Liberalism: How the Hoover-Roosevelt Debate Shapes the 21st Century* (Salem, MA: M&M Scrivener Press, 2007), 35–39.

27. Joseph Postell and Johnathan O'Neill, eds., *Toward an American Conservatism: Constitutional Conservatism during the Progressive Era* (New York: Palgrave Macmillan, 2013), 242.

28. Ibid.

29. Ibid., 243.

30. Lloyd, *Two Faces of Liberalism*, 38.

31. Herbert Hoover, *The Challenge to Liberty* (New York: C. Scribner's Sons, 1934), 54.

32. Herbert Hoover to Dr. William Starr Myers, January 8, 1938. Our gratitude to Dr. George H. Nash, who shared a copy of this letter with us.

33. Ibid.

34. Hoover, *Challenge to Liberty*, 54–55.

35. Charles A. Beard, *An Economic Interpretation of the Constitution of the United States* (New York: Macmillan, 1913).

36. John Dewey, *Individualism Old and New* (New York: Minton, Balch, 1930), 18.

37. Ibid., 36.

38. Ibid., 92.

39. Ibid., 103.

40. Ibid., 115.

41. Ibid., 107.

42. Ibid., 119–20.

43. Ibid., 127–28.

44. Ibid., 154–58.

45. Postell and O'Neill, *Toward an American Conservatism*, note 1, 235.

46. Ibid., note 2.

47. Gordon Lloyd and David Davenport, "The Two Phases of Herbert Hoover's Constitutional Conservatism," in *Toward an American Conservatism*, ed. Postell and O'Neill, 235–66.

48. Postell and O'Neill, *Toward an American Conservatism*, note 16, 238.

49. Ibid., 239.

50. Lloyd, *Two Faces of Liberalism*, 104–14.

51. Richard Norton Smith, *An Uncommon Man: The Triumph of Herbert Hoover* (New York: Simon and Schuster, 1984); William E. Leuchtenburg, *Herbert Hoover* (New York: Henry Holt and Company, 2009), 61.

52. Amity Shlaes, *The Forgotten Man: A New History of the Great Depression* (New York: HarperCollins, 2007), 148–49, 392; Murray N. Rothbard, "Hoover's Attack on Laissez-Faire," Mises Institute, April 12, 2008, https://mises.org /library/hoovers-attack-laissez-faire.

53. Michael A. Bernstein, *The Great Depression: Delayed Recovery and Economic Change in America, 1929–1939* (New York: Cambridge University Press, 1987), 207; Herbert Stein, *The Fiscal Revolution in America: Policy in Pursuit of Reality* (Washington, DC: AEI Press, 1990), 170.

54. Lloyd, *Two Faces of Liberalism*, 123.

55. Ickes, *New Democracy*, 26.

56. Gordon Lloyd and David Davenport, *The New Deal and Modern American Conservatism: A Defining Rivalry* (Stanford, CA: Hoover Institution Press, 2013), 20.

57. Yehoshua Arieli, *Individualism and Nationalism in American Ideology* (Cambridge, MA: Harvard University Press, 1964), 192.

58. Ibid., 346–347.

59. Ibid.

60. Wrobel, *End of American Exceptionalism*, 134.

61. Ibid., 135.

62. Ickes, *New Democracy*, 120–121.

63. Woodrow Wilson, "The Study of Administration," *Political Science Quarterly* 2 (1887): 197.

64. Ickes, *New Democracy*, 96.

65. Henry A. Wallace, *New Frontiers* (New York: Reynal and Hitchcock, 1934), 15.

66. Bellah et al., *Habits of the Heart*, 209.

67. Timothy Egan, "When FDR Found 'The Forgotten Man'," *New York Times*, August 28, 2008, http://www.nytimes.com/2008/08/28/opinion/28iht-edegan.1.15715387.html.

68. Lloyd, *Two Faces of Liberalism*, 107.

69. Wrobel, *End of American Exceptionalism*, 128.

70. John Halpin and Conor P. Williams, "The Progressive Intellectual Tradition in America," Center for American Progress, https://www.americanprogress .org/issues/progressive-movement/report/2010/04/14/7677/the-progressive -intellectual-tradition-in-america/.

71. Eric Rauchway, *The Great Depression and the New Deal: A Very Short Introduction* (New York: Oxford University Press, 2008), 70.

72. John Maynard Keynes, *Essays in Persuasion* (New York: Norton, 1963), 312–13.

73. John Stuart Mill, *Principles of Political Economy* (London: John William Parker, 1848), 334–35.

74. Jacob Viner, "The Intellectual History of Laissez Faire," *The Journal of Law and Economics* 3 (October 1960), 45.

75. Friedrich Hayek, *The Road to Serfdom* (Chicago: University of Chicago Press, 1944), 40–41.

76. Walter E. Weyl, *The New Democracy: An Essay on Certain Political and Economic Tendencies in the United States* (New York: Macmillan, 1912), 39.

77. Ickes, *New Democracy*, 31–32.

78. Wrobel, *End of American Exceptionalism*, 128.

79. Lloyd, *Two Faces of Liberalism*, 137.

CHAPTER THREE

RUGGED INDIVIDUALISM (BARELY) SURVIVES MODERNITY

FRANKLIN ROOSEVELT'S NEW DEAL wasted no time in building out a greatly enlarged federal government infrastructure that would curtail both the territory and the freedom of rugged individualism. If the meaning of democracy was now to include extensive federal programs for the forgotten man, then expansion of the federal infrastructure surely follows. There are several ways to measure the growth of the federal government and its effect on rugged individualism: the creation of new federal departments, the birth of new agencies, expanded regulations, new fields of federal responsibility, growth in size as measured by the number of employees and expenditures as a percentage of GDP (gross domestic product), etc. The New Deal moved aggressively on all fronts.

Federal Growth: History Tells an Interesting Story

The timing and growth of new federal departments tell an interesting story. In the beginning (1789), there were only three cabinet departments: War, State, and Treasury, corresponding to the primary responsibilities of the new federal government as the founders saw them. Even though the territory of the United States expanded enormously between the founding and the Civil War era—with the Northwest Ordinance, the Louisiana Purchase, the Florida Purchase, and land acquired through the Mexican War—the only cabinet department created to oversee the growth was the Department of the Interior (established in 1849). The Supreme Court also increased from seven members to nine during this time, and representation in both the House and the Senate grew as the population grew and new states were added.

It is not surprising that, with the end of the Civil War, the role of the federal government increased as it worked through what a post-slavery society in the South might look like. The Office of the Attorney General was moved out of the Executive Office of the President to its own cabinet-level Department of Justice (1870). The Thirteenth, Fourteenth, and Fifteenth amendments were passed, ending slavery and expanding the role of the federal government in the areas of civil rights and voting rights. As Herbert Hoover pointed out in his essay on "American Individualism," rugged individualism in the United States is accompanied by equality of opportunity, and this phase in the growth and reach of the federal government is both explained and justified by expanding opportunity in the aftermath of slavery and the Civil War. The Department of Agriculture was also established in that time frame (1862).

The Progressives—distrustful of free markets, the states, and rugged individualism—wanted to increase the regulatory role of the federal government in business. So the Departments of Commerce (1903) and Labor (1913) were created. When joined with Agriculture, the federal government now had a big say in what happened in the major sectors of the economy. Then, too, the Progressive Era saw the creation of major new regulatory agencies, such as the Interstate Commerce Commission (1887) and the Federal Reserve System (1913). Major antitrust laws were passed: the Sherman Act in 1890 and the Clayton Act in 1914. This phase of federal growth inserted Washington, D.C., into the capital-labor battles and hemmed in free markets and businesses with government regulation.

Then, too, came the Progressive constitutional amendments: the Sixteenth Amendment with its federal income tax, the Seventeenth allowing the direct election of US senators, the Eighteenth establishing Prohibition, and the Nineteenth giving women the right to vote, the last again expanding equality of opportunity. Overall, the Progressives aggressively inserted the federal government into business and free markets, expanding regulation at the expense of individualism, and illuminating the tension between rugged individualism and democracy.

But it was left to the New Deal to enact the largest expansion of the federal government in our history. Much of this was accomplished in the name of addressing a temporary economic emergency, but nearly all the expanded infrastructure became a permanent addition to the federal bureaucracy. Indeed, the New Deal has become the framework in which American domestic and economic policy operates even today, more than eighty years later. The New Deal was the first, and most important, of three revolutionary periods in modern times that have come to define the relationship between a growing federal government and the freedom of the rugged individual. Each of those three revolutions—Franklin Roosevelt's New Deal of the 1930s, Lyndon Johnson's Great Society in the 1960s, and the Reagan Revolution of the 1980s—marks a turning point in the evolving story of how the federal government's role has grown in such a way as to crowd out and limit rugged individualism.

The New Deal Revolution

In the first one hundred days of the New Deal in 1933, a vast array of emergency legislation was enacted. In all, some forty new administrative agencies, referred to by historians as the alphabet soup agencies, were formed in the first year of the New Deal. What the new measures had in common was a shift in power away from the people and their elected representatives in the Congress toward expert administrators in the executive branch. Roosevelt practiced what President Obama's former chief of staff,

Rahm Emanuel, later preached: "You never want a serious crisis to go to waste. . . . [It's] the opportunity to do things that you could not do before."[1]

The most sweeping law was the 1933 National Industrial Recovery Act, which began—as did its companion, the Agricultural Adjustment Act of 1933—by declaring a national emergency. It then delegated to the president alone the powers to "effectuate the purpose" of the law and to set "codes of fair competition." Republican Congressman Charles Eaton of New Jersey said at the time that this law was the New Deal's attempt "to remake the entire structure" of American capitalism.[2] Political scientist and historian Ira Katznelson explained the grand scale of the New Deal revolution: "In a decisive break with the old, the New Deal intentionally crafted not just a new set of policies but also new forms of institutional meaning, language, and possibility for a model that had been invented 150 years before," adding that it "retrofit[ted] capitalism and shap[ed] a welfare state."[3] While the Supreme Court later ruled that Congress's broad delegation of power to the executive branch was unconstitutional, much of the law itself remained.[4] The rugged individual thus became the regulated individual.

Another example of the New Deal revolution with contemporary application is Roosevelt's 1934 executive order creating the National Labor Relations Board. One might assume that a president could not unilaterally create a board with extensive powers over collective bargaining, labor relations, and labor elections, but Roosevelt felt that the National Industrial Recovery Act was sufficiently broad to authorize this. The president concluded that "this Executive Order . . . marks a great step forward in administrative efficiency and more important in labor matters," allowing the president, through this new board, to have the "machinery for adjusting labor relations . . . be clarified." To those concerned with the extent of the president's use of executive orders today, this is a powerful precedent, and to those worried about the health of rugged individualism, a discouraging one, with the president now using the emergency legislation of the economic crisis to establish even greater federal regulation of labor, management, and the marketplace.

It is surprising to look back and see that Roosevelt carried out his revolution without even using two primary sources of power. First, there were no new cabinet departments created by Roosevelt, but instead scores of executive agencies, boards, and commissions. Second, there were no constitutional amendments to effect or codify the New Deal revolution. The only constitutional amendment of that era was one following Roosevelt's unprecedented twelve-year presidency to limit the president to two terms. Instead there were constitutional interpretations, by both Roosevelt and the courts. In Roosevelt's Constitution Day speech on September 17, 1937, he asserted that the Constitution is "a layman's document, not a lawyer's contract." But Roosevelt's constitution was not about American individualism and liberty but, as he said in that speech, about meeting the "insistence of the great mass of our people that economic and social security and the standard of American living be raised . . . to levels which the people know our resources justify." Therefore, he added, we cannot "seriously be alarmed" when people use "legalistic phrases" to "cry 'unconstitutional' at every effort to better the condition of our people." To Roosevelt, the Constitution was an evolving document and needed to catch up to the social and economic needs of his "forgotten man," not be caught up in legalism and individual rights. This, of course, continues to be part of the constitutional debate today between "originalists" and those who believe in a "living constitution."

The New Deal relegated rugged individualism to the back bench and focused public policy instead on the forgotten man. In fact, the rugged individual was now part of the problem, tied with laissez-faire economics and the fat cats on Wall Street, and not part of the solution. In the name of an economic emergency, Roosevelt expanded and redirected the federal government toward massive intervention in the economy and in every kind of federal policy. Only recently, the US Supreme Court found itself asking whether New Deal policies still in effect concerning raisins still made sense, with even dissenting Justice Sonia Sotomayor acknowledging that the price support law "may be outdated and by some lights downright silly."[5] It was a complete revolution away from individualism, constitutionalism, and free markets toward government growth and intervention in favor of the forgotten man.

Before leaving the New Deal, however, we should acknowledge one small step for rugged individualism: the blended approach that left room for both the rugged individual and the forgotten man in addressing Social Security and retirement. The 1935 Social Security Act was to "furnish financial assistance . . . to aged needy individuals."[6] The definition of "aged" was provided in the Act: age sixty-five. But "needy" was a more difficult term, calling forth a sliding scale test based upon total wages earned in which higher wage contributions received smaller percentage returns. To pay for these services, a tax on employee wages and an excise tax on employers were established.

In a sense, the formula for Social Security established a two-track system, one for the rugged individual and one for the forgotten man. As historian Edward Berkowitz described it, "Public and private pensions expanded together and the compatibility of the two became one of Social Security's celebrated virtues."[7] The rugged individual who can take care of himself must nevertheless pay into the system and may only receive back a portion of his investment. On a percentage basis, the forgotten man was entitled to receive more. But the rugged individual could have private retirement funds alongside his Social Security payments, and the government would later (in the 1970s) allow certain of those funds to grow on a tax-deferred basis. It was not one-size-fits-all as we would later see, for example, in the case of Obamacare. And this synthesis provides one useful way to think about the rugged individual in public policy: carve out a track that makes sense for those who can take care of themselves and a different track—a safety net—for those who cannot.

By now, of course, that distinction has become blurred in Social Security. As Social Security has evolved since 1935, it has become less a safety net and more of an entitlement for both the rugged individual and the forgotten man. Both have merged into a new class: the entitled man. So a promising synthesis in which the rugged individual and the forgotten man were each addressed separately by the Social Security policy has ended up compromised, with everyone now an entitled man, and the costs have sky-rocketed well beyond the ability of the system to pay them.

The Postwar Transition

With the end of World War II and the death of Franklin Roosevelt, one might have expected the postwar world to see the massive New Deal and wartime growth of the federal government cut back. Indeed, Herbert Hoover himself was brought out of retirement in 1947 to head up the first Hoover Commission for the reorganization of the executive branch of government, a project promising to be not merely an organizational exercise but an actual reduction in the role of the federal government. But with the surprise election of Democrat Harry Truman in 1948, the wind came out of those sails and the Hoover Commission settled for rearranging the offices rather than returning to a form of democratic republicanism more compatible with the founders.[8]

When Dwight D. Eisenhower, a Republican, was elected president in 1952, there was new hope among many for a reduction in the size and role of the federal government, and Herbert Hoover was called upon to lead a second Hoover Commission. But once again, a new president turned out to be cool toward declaring war on the federal programs of the New Deal. Eisenhower seemed to acknowledge the political difficulty of rolling back popular entitlement programs and was willing to accept the social safety net constructed by the New Deal.[9] When James Reston of the *New York Times* evaluated Eisenhower's first term in 1956, he concluded it was "surely one of the great paradoxes of recent American political history" that Republicans had "swallowed" the New Deal measures without attempting to repeal a single one.[10] And this becomes part of the larger story of government incursions into the life of the rugged individual: some become accepted, as Eisenhower did with Social Security and other aspects of the safety net, while others remain contentious.

Indeed, Eisenhower proceeded to build the federal government in new directions, establishing the new Department of Health, Education, and Welfare, reorganizing the Defense Department, creating the National Aeronautics and Space Administration, and constructing tens of thousands of miles of interstate highway across the country. It is symbolic and fitting that the large federal executive office building next to the White House is named for Eisenhower. Still, Eisenhower saw the dangers of big government allied with big business, warning in his farewell address about "the military-industrial complex." He also saw danger to the rugged individual, highlighting the "solitary inventor, tinkering in his shop, [who] has been overshadowed by task forces of scientists" funded by the federal government.

President John F. Kennedy, in his brief term, proceeded to push the federal government into civil rights, the exploration of space, and other aspects of the "new frontier" he advanced. Ironically, Progressives had earlier pronounced that the American frontier, and with it rugged individualism, had disappeared, but Kennedy saw an optimistic and compelling "new frontier." In his inaugural address he famously called upon Americans to "ask not what your country can do for you—ask what you can do for your country." But classical liberal economist Milton Friedman objected to Kennedy's challenge, calling it both "paternalistic" and "organismic." Friedman, a leading figure of twentieth-century conservatism, urged Americans not to be lulled into accepting Kennedy's seductive challenge, saying that instead Americans should ask: "What can I and my compatriots do through government . . . to protect our freedoms?"[11] As Friedman would often explain, the most important part of that was limiting the government's power and reach over the individual.

The Great Society Revolution

Thrust into office by the death of President Kennedy in 1963, and elected by a landslide in 1964, Lyndon Johnson had a lot of political capital to spend. And, as the long-time Senate majority leader, he knew how to get things done in the Capitol. As a consequence, despite being weighed down by the advancing conflict in Vietnam, Johnson carried out a massive domestic agenda he called the Great Society. Capturing the large Johnson personality and expansive vision of government, he often said at campaign stops, "We're in favor of a lot of things and against mighty few."[12]

One of the major contributions of Johnson's Great Society was an expanded definition of the forgotten man to include not only the poor but racial minorities, children, and anyone else who had been left behind by society. In this sense, Johnson provided a vision for who should be helped and what should be done by government in a Great Society. His landmark speech at the University of Michigan on May 22, 1964, best captured LBJ's notion of the Great Society. He made it clear that just having wealth did not make a great society: a great and happy society needed to end poverty and racial injustice. But to Johnson, that was "just the beginning." Johnson argued that three projects would comprise the heart of his domestic effort: (1) making the cities and urban areas great; (2) addressing environmental issues in the countryside (water, food, air, parks); and (3) making the educational system excellent so that everyone had a promising future. Not only did the Great Society build on the New Deal, but Johnson sought to out-Roosevelt his mentor and hero if he could.

In a day now when relatively little legislation is actually passed by Congress and signed by the president, the scale of the Great Society is difficult to comprehend. In total, the Great Society agenda comprised some 435 bills, one for every member of the House.[13] This staggering volume of legislative achievement included such major measures as Medicare, Medicaid, the Civil Rights Act of 1964, the Voting Rights Act of 1965, the Fair Housing Act of 1968, the Elementary and Secondary Education Act, Head Start, Model Cities, and the Truth-in-Lending Act. A new cabinet department for Housing and Urban Development was created.

Political scientist James Q. Wilson later observed that part of the permanent change effected by the Great Society was "lowering the legitimacy barrier" for federal government action.[14] Previously there had been a serious argument over whether the federal government had the constitutional legitimacy to act in domestic matters such as welfare, education, urban renewal, etc. But, as Wilson said, thanks to the Great Society, that barrier has fallen and "political conflict takes a very different form. New programs need not await the advent of a crisis or an extraordinary majority because no program is any longer 'new'—it is seen, rather, as an extension, a modification, or an enlargement of something the government is already doing."[15]

In order to accomplish his agenda, Johnson employed what he described as "creative federalism." In a November 11, 1966, memorandum to his senior officials, Johnson urged joint action on major problems "worked out and planned in a cooperative spirit with those chief officials of state, county, and local governments who are answerable to their citizens."[16] Although the federal government role was expanded to address state and local problems such as education and welfare, this would largely be accomplished by categorical grants, often bypassing the states and going directly to neighborhood organizations or nonprofit groups. Grants-in-aid were the preferred tool for this, with federal grant programs growing from 132 in 1960 to 379 by 1967. Similarly, funding for those grants grew from $8.6 billion in 1963 to $20.3 billion by 1969.[17] For the rugged individual, then, the vast growth of the federal government and its ever deeper involvement in people's lives was somewhat mitigated by channeling funds into local and community groups. But many of these local and state partners would prove to be unreliable and uneven in their approaches, so the federal role lasted whereas the state and local partnerships often did not.

Medicare and Medicaid provide a classic case study in how creative federalism was intended to work in the Great Society. Rather than federalize health care entirely, Medicare sought to work alongside the existing system of private health insurance, with private doctors and hospitals. As Robert Ball, the Social Security commissioner during the Johnson administration, put it, Medicare simply "accepted the going system of the delivery of care and the program structure was molded on previous private insurance arrangements."[18] Health insurance for the working population would continue to be provided by private insurance companies and community health plans such as Blue Cross and Blue Shield. Medicare and Medicaid, established through an amendment to the Social Security Act, would provide medical insurance for the elderly in a kind of safety-net system. As a result, even this sweeping law left room for the rugged individual and the forgotten man to coexist, the former retaining his private or employment-provided insurance and the latter benefiting from the government-created safety net. Even this synthesis, however, was not a massive victory for the rugged individual. Ball later acknowledged that this was only done because otherwise politics would prevent the passage of the Medicare and Medicaid legislation—the goal all along had been to federalize medical care.[19]

Likewise, the Great Society's approach to poverty at least held out some hope for rugged individualism. Johnson made it clear that his approach was not cash handouts to the poor, but rather empowering the poor to be qualified and able to find work. The Declaration of Purpose of the war on poverty legislation said the program would work by "opening to everyone the opportunity for education and training, the opportunity to work, and the opportunity to live in decency and dignity." In the end, Johnson's reach exceeded his grasp. Poverty, of course, was not eliminated, and the Office of Economic Opportunity that led the war against it was eliminated in the next decade. Twenty years later, Charles Murray would argue that the Great Society's anti-poverty programs actually abetted rather than ameliorated it.[20] Joseph Califano Jr., Johnson's chief domestic policy advisor, acknowledged that, during the Great Society era, "the Government simply got into too many nooks and crannies of American life."[21] The notion that the federal government can and should do everything for everyone not only undercut individual liberty but, as a practical matter, did not work.

The Transition of the 1970s

It is not the case that every time a Democrat was elected president the federal government grew, and whenever a Republican came into office the federal government shrank. In fact, between the end of the Great Society, when Lyndon Johnson did not seek reelection in 1968, and the election of Ronald Reagan in 1980, the federal government continued to grow in both size and reach under two Republican presidents, Richard Nixon and Gerald Ford, and one Democrat, Jimmy Carter.

Nixon added new federal agencies—the Department of Natural Resources, the Environmental Protection Agency, the Council on Environmental Quality, and the Occupational Safety and Health Administration—and enacted one of the most sweeping federal environmental laws, the Clean Air Act of 1970. Rather than cut taxes, as conservatives would have wished, Nixon redirected federal money toward states and municipalities. Declaring "I am now a Keynesian," Nixon completed Franklin Roosevelt's earlier initiative to take America off the gold standard, and he also imposed federal wage and price controls to combat inflation in 1971. He even proposed a Family Assistance Program that would have guaranteed a minimum welfare payment for every American, but that was defeated in the Senate. In short, Nixon presided over a significant expansion of the federal welfare and administrative state.

President Ford was left to clean up the Watergate mess and to deal with inflation when wage and price controls did not do the job. And President Carter's term was dominated by economic concerns—both inflation and unemployment—an energy crisis, and the Iran hostage situation. Carter talked about smaller government but, in the end, pursued big government policies to address tough problems. His primary organizational accomplishment was to split the former Department of Health, Education, and Welfare into two cabinet-level departments, one for Health and Human Services and a separate Department of Education. The latter empowered far greater intrusion by the federal government into education at all levels. In summary, the 1970s were a continuation of the New Deal and Great Society eras.

The Reagan Revolution

Ronald Reagan had a very different understanding of the federal government and its role than his modern predecessors. He first articulated his view on the national stage in a major televised address called "A Time for Choosing" during Barry Goldwater's failed campaign for the presidency in 1964. If the University of Michigan address on the Great Society was Johnson's case statement for his presidency, Reagan's philosophy was best stated in this message. He began the domestic policy portion of this message, delivered on October 27, 1964, by looking at the failure of the economic pillar of the American system. Who is going to pay for all the Great Society programs? Reagan asked. He was also troubled by the assumption that the federal government is the level and the executive is the branch to fix America's domestic policy. "No government ever voluntarily reduces itself in size," Reagan said. "So government's programs, once launched, never disappear. Actually, a government bureau is the nearest thing to eternal life we'll ever see on this earth."

Adding more specifics, Reagan noted that the individual income tax rate was too high, the federal budget had not been balanced twenty-eight of the last thirty-four years, and the federal debt limit had been raised three times in the last twelve months. "We have accepted Social Security," Reagan acknowledged, but the federal workforce was too large and "proliferating bureaus with their thousands of regulations have cost us many of our constitutional rights." As a consequence, Reagan concluded, "a perversion has taken place," our natural rights "are now considered to be a dispensation of government," and freedom has become fragile. Echoes of Herbert Hoover's observation in the 1932 election campaign—this is not a choice between two men but two philosophies of government—could be heard in the Reagan address. Reagan clearly saw that big government meant less freedom for the individual.

When elected president in 1980, Reagan included this now-famous statement in his first inaugural address: "Government is not the solution to our problem; government is the problem." Noting that government "has no power except that granted it by the people," Reagan said it was "time to check and reverse the growth of government which shows signs of having grown beyond the consent of the governed." In a news conference on August 12, 1986, Reagan said: "The most terrifying words in the English language are, 'I'm from the government and I'm here to help.'" Concluding his presidency, he said, "Man is not free unless government is limited," in his 1988 farewell speech. But Reagan found actually reversing the trend of government growth to be a major challenge. He did succeed in cutting taxes—initially a 23 percent across-the-board cut of individual tax rates phased in over three years, followed later by another cut. In total, he cut the top income tax rate from 70 percent to 28 percent. But under Reagan the federal workforce grew modestly and the national debt went from $907 billion in 1980 to $2.6 trillion in 1988. Some of this increase was a further commitment to national defense and some was the difficulty of getting spending cuts through Congress.

In addition to tax cuts, Reagan made progress in the "devolution" of some federal responsibilities back to state and local governments and in deregulating the airlines and banking. He sought to return financial responsibility for more than sixty federal programs for low-income households to state and local government, funded at least in part by federal grants.[22] Much of this "New Federalism" or "devolution" did not actually become law, although the federal budgets under Reagan nevertheless reduced funding for these programs. There was talk of eliminating the federal Department of Education, but this did not occur. Instead, a major national study on "A Nation at Risk" in 1983 led to expanded federal leadership in education.

Still, in addition to tax cuts and some devolution, Reagan's philosophical and rhetorical attack on big government and his defense of individual freedom provided valuable underpinning for the continued importance of American rugged individualism. In his book *The Age of Reagan: The Conservative Counterrevolution, 1980–1989*, Steven F. Hayward argued that Reagan restored much of the American founding that had been lost or forgotten. We agree. Even some of his foreign affairs and national defense speeches were fundamentally about individual freedom. His famous Berlin speech on June 12, 1987, with its challenge, "Mr. Gorbachev, tear down this wall," was fundamentally about the ideal of individual freedom. In his 1982 Westminster speech, he warned about the threat to "human freedom by the enormous power of the modern state." And in his 1988 State of the Union address, he said that "limited government" is the "best way of ensuring personal liberty." This clear link between personal liberty and American individualism, on the one hand, and limited government on the other, was an important contribution.

It is not too much to claim that Reagan rhetorically re-centered the nation in its understanding of individualism and democracy. Rather than asking first what government can do to solve problems, Reagan asked the classic "rugged individualism" question: what can the individual do? If he decided that a matter was properly addressed by government, rather than left to the individual, Reagan would then turn to questions of federalism: which level of government and which branch? All of this reordered the thinking of conservatives and of the nation itself. Reagan's sunny optimism made the individualism and limited government case with greater effectiveness than the sometimes dour Calvin Coolidge or Herbert Hoover of an earlier era or the harder Western persona of Barry Goldwater. One should not underestimate this rhetorical and spiritual reawakening and re-centering accomplished by Ronald Reagan. Indeed, one of the questions to be asked at the end of the Reagan Revolution or the New Deal is not just whether the programmatic outcome was good—whether unemployment or the size of government was tamed—but the articulation of the proper relationship between the government and the people.

Philosophical Debates about American Individualism

As individualism versus collectivism played out on the political and policy scene, there were also relevant debates about it in the realm of philosophy and ideas. Two of these debates especially informed the larger public policy approach to the subject. One might best be understood as coming from the world of political economy, with two of the leading contenders being libertarian-conservative Milton Friedman, representing the importance of individual liberty, and political scientist Michael Harrington, standing for many of the socialist or collectivist ideals of the student radical movement of the 1960s. A second round of conversations about individualism in America was triggered by sociologist Robert Bellah and political scientist Robert Putnam in their respective books, *Habits of the Heart* and *Bowling Alone*.

In Milton Friedman's introduction to the fiftieth anniversary edition of Friedrich Hayek's *Road to Serfdom*,[23] Friedman praised Hayek for capturing the timeless choice facing society: collectivism and central direction (serfdom) versus individualism and voluntary cooperation (freedom). Hayek had understood that there was a road to freedom that had been abandoned, pointing to the German intellectuals of the 1870s who felt central planning was needed and left the road to freedom in favor of socialism and ultimately totalitarianism. Hayek sought to reintroduce the alternative of individualism, arguing that central planning led to bad policy and also resulted in coercion.

Friedman argued that political freedom, which was embraced widely in America, depended on maintaining economic and social freedom as well.[24] He argued, like Hayek, that there were really only two choices: (1) a relatively free market; or (2) government control of the economy. The mixed solution, which became known later as the Nordic or Scandinavian model, was unworkable. First Friedman, then Goldwater, and later Reagan revived the notion of rugged individualism, establishing a free and responsible society as a preferable alternative to collectivism. Whereas Hayek had been fighting European socialism, Friedman was battling the regulatory state of the American Progressives. Both provided an important foundation for individualism.

In addition, Friedman offered two ways of measuring how the size and reach of government correspondingly reduced the level of freedom enjoyed by the individual. One measure is government spending as a percentage of national income. His goal was 10 percent for all government spending (not just federal), which he noted was actually in practice in 1928, prior to the Great Depression. What concerned Friedman was that the percentage rose to 20 percent during the New Deal era and up to 36 percent by the time Ronald Reagan came to office. Following the Reagan Revolution, the percentage hovered near the 34 percent range for the next twenty years. By 2008, however, it rose to 40 percent.[25] By Friedman's accounting, then, the Reagan Revolution at least put a brake on government growth.

Friedman's second test is the amount and kind of government regulation over people's daily lives. He listed fourteen government regulations that he claimed were inconsistent with a free society in 1962: parity price support, tariffs, output control, rent control, minimum wage laws, industrial regulation (Interstate Commerce Commission), speech regulation (Federal Communications Commission), social security, licensing, public housing, military conscription, national parks, the US Post Office, and toll roads.[26] Not listed is education, though he devoted a lot of time to arguing against the government monopoly in education, being an early proponent of vouchers. By now, this list from 1962 could be multiplied many times over (see chapter 4).

During the 1960s, an alternative economic view was developed and promulgated by student radicals and intellectuals, one that would further undercut the notion of American individualism in favor of greater collectivism. And, as in the Progressive Era, this would largely be undertaken by reducing individualism to purely economic notions of greed. A good starting point is the Port Huron Statement, a 1962 manifesto developed by Students for a Democratic Society (SDS). In it, the so-called New Left laid out how the relative comfort of the childhoods of college students had now been undone by racism, nuclear threats, the Cold War, poverty, corrupt capitalism, and the decline of American values. The statement actually purported to support a certain kind of anti-establishment individualism, one that would not fall into "egoism." But in fact it pointed to a reinventing of American society, foreign policy, labor relations, university governance, and social structure around New Left principles.

In the same year, 1962, Michael Harrington, a political scientist, activist, and socialist, published the influential book, *The Other America*, with its sweeping indictment of government policy toward poverty. Indeed, Harrington's book clashed directly with another intellectual of the time, Assistant Secretary of Labor Daniel Patrick Moynihan, who developed the framework for Johnson's War on Poverty. Whereas Moynihan thought that family structure among the poor, especially the black poor, was the fundamental problem, Harrington argued that it was all about unemployment, underemployment, and poor housing. The problem was in the very culture of poverty, Harrington said, demanding a cultural change.[27] Harrington argued that central planning was needed to develop housing and jobs and infuse billions of dollars into social investment in order to solve the problem. Instead, he said, "The great opportunity for social change since the New Deal was sacrificed to the tragedy in Vietnam."[28]

To Harrington and the student radicals of the 1960s, the welfare state was not enough to save the poor and minorities from the harshness of market capitalism. The welfare state only made the poor into wards of the state; it wasn't built to address the hopelessness and desperation of poverty. We need social security, housing, and a comprehensive medical program for all, Harrington said.[29] The appendices to the book track the ongoing data about poverty since 1962, supporting Harrington's claim that the same people were poor in 1970 who had been poor in 1960. He felt the War on Poverty had really done nothing.

It is little wonder, then, that Johnson's Great Society revolution had unraveled by 1968. Under attack from Friedman, Goldwater, and those favoring greater individual rights and less government from the right, and the New Left demanding a government transformation well beyond the welfare state, Johnson was very much caught in the middle of a heated war. Then, too, came his unpopular buildup and failure abroad in the Vietnam War. What the 1960s essentially added to the debate about rugged individualism and the 1930s welfare state was a new critique from the left that the welfare state had not gone far enough. This debate very much continues today.

The Sociological Debate about Individualism Also Informs Public Policy

Another philosophical debate about individualism, this one involving primarily sociological analysis, addressed individualism itself, specifically whether it was a kind of selfishness that undercut the social cohesion necessary for a free republic. In that sense, the debate reached back at least to Tocqueville, who had pointed out that American individualism was different from European understandings of this idea. It was based on self-interest "rightly understood," a self-interest that included a commitment to others.

Robert Bellah, a sociologist at the University of California at Berkeley, and several of his colleagues published *Habits of the Heart* during the Reagan Revolution in 1985. The subtitle of the book raises its core concern: "Individualism and Commitment in American Life." In the preface to the book, the authors warn that American individualism "may have grown cancerous—it may be destroying those social integuments that Tocqueville saw as moderating its more destructive potentialities, that it may be threatening the survival of freedom itself."[30] In the glossary of the book, the authors acknowledge that individualism carries at least two meanings: (1) "a belief in the inherent dignity and, indeed, sacredness of the human person," and (2) "a belief that the individual has a primary reality whereas society is a second-order."[31] The second understanding—that the individual is primary and voluntarily consents to participation in society in various ways—is the essence of American individualism. But Bellah and his colleagues, fearing the rise of the selfish French "individualism," call for the rise of communitarian or collective forces, apparently ignoring Tocqueville's understanding that Americans already do participate voluntarily and extensively.

In 2000, Harvard political scientist Robert Putnam published *Bowling Alone: The Collapse and Revival of American Community*. Putnam spoke of the need for "social capital" to make a nation work well, including both what he called bonding capital (relationships with people who are alike) and bridging capital (relationships with different kinds of people). The title of his book is drawn from the demise of bowling leagues, a minimal form of civic engagement, showing that individualism has threatened the formation of vital social capital. Putnam's work triggered important debates about whether social capital has actually declined or whether earlier forms of community engagement, such as Elks Clubs and bowling leagues, had simply given way to new forms of community and civic engagement.[32]

Fundamental to any debate about individualism versus communitarianism or collectivism is one's understanding of individualism itself. The battle always seems to result from an effort by communitarians and collectivists to define individualism narrowly, in a selfish, self-interested, even economically advantaged way. Then supporters of individualism respond: No, it's not that limited; it must be "rightly understood" (Tocqueville); it incorporates equality of opportunity (Hoover); it leaves men free to consent, free to associate voluntarily. Stanford political scientist Francis Fukuyama sees another useful distinction: Americans may be anti-statists, but that is not the same as hostility to community.[33] As Fukuyama pointed out, "The same Americans who are against state regulation, taxation, oversight, and ownership of productive resources can be extraordinarily cooperative and sociable in their companies, voluntary associations, churches, newspapers, universities, and the like."[34] Americans also tend to be very loyal and committed to family, which is an extension beyond mere individualism. So perhaps it is a certain *kind* of forced community, community demanded by the state, that Americans resist, preferring instead to start with individualism and consent to join associations of various kinds. Indeed, Americans are widely known for their philanthropy, volunteerism, church membership, and so on. Do these things not count to the collectivists? As sociologist Seymour Martin Lipset rightly observed, "[I]n America, individualism *strengthens* the bonds of civil society rather than weakens them."[35]

Conclusion

Rugged individualism in the modern era became a tug of war carried out on philosophical, economic, political, and policy grounds. Presidents Franklin Roosevelt and Lyndon Johnson concluded that rugged individualism had left millions of people behind economically and sought to extend the reach of the federal government to assist the forgotten man by constructing a welfare safety net and developing scores of new government programs. By the 1980s, Ronald Reagan won the presidency, arguing that the federal government had grown too large and intrusive and needed to be trimmed back to leave room for more individual liberty, though he found the actual reduction in the size and role of government to be a major challenge.

Despite efforts by the Progressives, the New Left, and other communitarians and collectivists to kill American rugged individualism, it managed to survive, if barely. Although Americans want to help those in need, there remains a preference for individual and voluntary action, in part because growing federal government programs have not seemed to solve the problems. As Tocqueville and others have observed, Americans have their own particular form of individualism that they are not prepared to give up. As the sociologist Herbert Gans put it, "virtually all sectors of the [American] population" continue to pursue individualism, but it "is hardly separation from other people. It is to live out their lives in freedom and engagement with small parts of society, starting with the family, while participating in a wide range of voluntary activities to assist others."[36]

Notes

1. Gerald F. Seib, "In Crisis, Opportunity for Obama," *Wall Street Journal*, November 21, 2008, http://www.wsj.com/articles/SB122721278056345271.

2. Ira Katznelson, *Fear Itself: The New Deal and the Origins of Our Time* (New York: Liveright, 2013), 238.

3. Ibid., 6, 36.

4. *A.L.A. Schechter Poultry Corp. v. United States*, 295 US 495, 55 S. Ct. 837, 79 L. Ed. 1570 (1935).

5. *Horne v. Department of Agriculture*, 576 US, no. 14–275 (2015).

6. Ibid., 216.

7. Edward Berkowitz, "Medicare: The Great Society's Enduring National Health Care Program," in *The Great Society and the High Tide of Liberalism*, ed. Sidney M. Milkis and Jerome M. Mileur (Boston: University of Massachusetts Press, 2005), 335.

8. See Joanna L. Grisinger, *The Unwieldy American State: Administrative Politics since the New Deal* (New York: Cambridge University Press, 2012).

9. Ibid., 199.

10. James Reston, "Eisenhower's Four Years: An Evaluation of the Republican Administration in a Complex World," *New York Times*, July 22, 1956.

11. Milton Friedman, *Capitalism and Freedom* (Chicago: University of Chicago Press, 1962), 1–3.

12. Theodore H. White, *The Making of the President 1964* (New York: New American Library, 1966), 413.

13. David Shribman, "Lyndon Johnson: Means and Ends, and What His Presidency Means in the End," in *The Great Society and the High Tide of Liberalism*, ed. Milkis and Mileur, note 8, 239.

14. James Q. Wilson, "American Politics: Then and Now," *Commentary*, February 1979, 41.

15. Ibid.

16. Lyndon B. Johnson, "Memorandum on the Need for 'Creative Federalism' through Cooperation with State and Local Officials," November 11, 1966, in *The American Presidency Project*, ed. Gerhard Peters and John T. Woolley, http://www.presidency.ucsb.edu/ws/?pid=28023.

17. Berkowitz, "Medicare," note 7, 323.

18. Ibid.

19. Ibid., 322.

20. Charles Murray, *Losing Ground: American Social Policy, 1950–1980* (Philadelphia: Basic Books, 1984).

21. David E. Rosenbaum, "20 Years Later, the Great Society Flourishes," *New York Times*, April 17, 1985, http://www.nytimes.com/1985/04/17/us/20-years-later-the-great-society-flourishes.html?pagewanted=all.

22. John M. Quigley and Daniel L. Rubinfeld, "Federalism and Reductions in the Federal Budget," *National Tax Journal* 49, no. 2 (June 1996): 189–302.

23. Friedrich Hayek, *The Road to Serfdom: Fiftieth Anniversary Edition* (Chicago: University of Chicago Press, 1994).

24. Friedman, *Capitalism and Freedom*, 7–21.

25. http://www.usgovernmentspending.com/total_spending_chart.

26. Friedman, *Capitalism and Freedom*, 35–36.

27. Michael Harrington, *The Other America: Poverty in the United States* (New York: Touchstone, 1962), 79.

28. Ibid., 205.

29. Ibid., 167.

30. Robert N. Bellah, Richard Madsen, William M. Sullivan, Ann Swidler, and Steven M. Tipton, *Habits of the Heart: Individualism and Commitment in American Life* (Berkeley, CA: University of California Press, 2007), xlviii.

31. Ibid., 334.

32. See David Davenport and Hanna Skandera, "Civic Associations," in *Never a Matter of Indifference: Sustaining Virtue in a Free Republic*, ed. Peter Berkowitz (Stanford, CA: Hoover Institution Press, 2003).

33. Francis Fukuyama, *Trust: The Social Virtues and the Creation of Prosperity* (New York: The Free Press, 1995), 51.

34. Ibid.

35. Seymour Martin Lipset, *American Exceptionalism: A Double-Edged Sword* (New York: W.W. Norton, 1996), 277 (emphasis original). See also Robert Wuthnow, *Acts of Compassion: Caring for Others and Helping Ourselves* (Princeton, NJ: Princeton University Press, 1992), 22.

36. Herbert J. Gans, *Middle American Individualism* (New York: The Free Press, 1988), 1–4.

CHAPTER FOUR

RUGGED INDIVIDUALISM HANGS IN THE BALANCE TODAY

D ESPITE HEAVY ATTACKS and declarations that its time has passed, American rugged individualism still survives. In some eras, such as the Reagan years, it has been foundational while at other times, such as the Progressive Era, it was on life support. President Barack Obama, much more attuned to communitarian or collectivist ideals than to rugged individualism, has nevertheless acknowledged its continued existence and its importance to the American psyche. In his famous speech in Osawatomie, Kansas, in 2011 launching his crusade on income inequality, for example, Obama acknowledged that "rugged individualism and our healthy skepticism of too much government" are "in America's DNA," but went on to say that "it doesn't work."[1] More recently, in the context of health care reform, Obama said in 2015 that "rugged individualism defines America," quickly adding, however, that it has always been "bound by a set of shared values."[2] So even Obama, much as one senses he might prefer not to, feels bound to connect with—and limit—the continuing ideal of American rugged individualism.

Senator Cory Booker of New Jersey reflected the Left's discomfort with rugged individualism in his speech to the Democratic National Convention on July 25, 2016. While Booker said, "I respect and value the ideals of rugged individualism," he nevertheless proceeded to attack it, noting that rugged individualism did not defeat the British, get us to the moon, build highways, or map the human genome. All those things, Booker emphasized, were done "together." But as we have seen, rugged individuals have often worked together, from wagon trains across the West in an earlier day to building houses through Habitat for Humanity today. The key is that Americans have been free to consent to these cooperative activities. But as was clear in his speech and others at the convention, what the Democrats seek is not more individual liberty and collaborative activity, but more federal government control, a far cry from his claim to "respect . . . rugged individualism."[3]

Today, rugged individualism is in a fight for its life on two battle-grounds: in the policy realm and in the intellectual world of ideas that may lead to new policies. Increasingly, policy is changed in America when intellectuals develop ideas that become a kind of conventional wisdom that, in turn, is incorporated into new policies and laws. Scientists began talking about the dangers of climate change, and then Al Gore jumped on the bandwagon, popularizing a new conventional wisdom that action was needed to protect the planet from, first, global warming and then climate change. Economist Thomas Piketty and others began talking about the rise of income inequality, and soon enough, President Obama argued for a new set of domestic priorities around the growing conventional wisdom that something needed to be done about income inequality. As Thomas Sowell pointed out in his book *Intellectuals and Society*, intellectuals play the increasingly important role of creating "a climate of opinion" or a "vision" that serves as a "general framework for the way particular issues and events . . . are perceived" and then "discussed and ultimately acted upon by those with political power."[4]

In the realm of ideas pertaining to rugged individualism, the work of two contemporary intellectuals seems especially important: French econo-mist Thomas Piketty and American historian Howard Zinn. Although Zinn died in 2010, his work lives on through his influential textbook,

A People's History of the United States, taught in high school and college history courses around the nation.[5] His ideas about the founding of the nation right on through his positions on governance and leadership today have been highly influential in creating a narrative that challenges American rugged individualism. Similarly Thomas Piketty's sweeping book, *Capital in the Twenty-First Century*, has laid the groundwork for modern thinking about income inequality and is the basis of a great deal of policy discussion.[6] Finally, from the world of ideas comes a set of books by law professors and political scientists questioning the American founding and Constitution, books that are also laying the groundwork for policy proposals that would impact rugged individualism. An examination of these books and ideas will provide an early-stage reading on the state of play of American rugged individualism today.

Then from the world of policy, clearly the most sweeping and important new law enacted under President Obama's leadership is the Affordable Care Act. This is at once the first truly major expansion of the welfare state since the Great Society of the 1960s and the most comprehensive federalization of a new field. It is also an interesting policy case study since it has been visited several times in the modern era: in the 1960s, again in the Clinton years, to some degree by President George W. Bush, and finally under President Obama. A second major policy area that has been the subject of considerable activity in the modern era is K–12 education. First came No Child Left Behind during the George W. Bush administration, then President Obama's Race to the Top, and finally the new Every Student Succeeds Act of 2015. From these case studies, then, in both the intellectual and policy fields, we may draw some conclusions about the current health and likely future of American rugged individualism.

Rugged Individualism and Obamacare

The primary legislative accomplishment of President Obama's two terms has been the enactment of the Affordable Care Act (ACA, or Obamacare, as it is popularly known). It is the most sweeping and important domestic policy since Lyndon Johnson's enactment of Medicare and Medicaid in the Great Society, which in turn built upon the Social Security safety net of Franklin Roosevelt's New Deal. It would be useful, therefore, to see how rugged individualism fares under Obamacare as a signal for its continuing viability in domestic policy.

It is worth recalling the roots of national health care, since the idea has been around for at least a hundred years. When Theodore Roosevelt ran for president as a Progressive, the party platform in 1912 included a commitment to the following provision: "The protection of home life against the hazards of sickness, irregular employment and old age through the adoption of a system of social insurance." Further, the platform called for "the union of all the existing agencies of the Federal Government dealing with public health into a single national health service." In his State of the Union address in 1944, President Franklin Roosevelt outlined what he called "a second Bill of Rights," among which was "the right to adequate medical care and the opportunity to achieve and enjoy good health," although he was not able to implement this. President Truman proposed a national health insurance plan to Congress, but it was not passed.

As noted in chapter 3, President Johnson's enactment of Medicare and Medicaid left room for both the rugged individual and the forgotten man. Those able to work and choose their own approach to health insurance could continue to buy individual health insurance or not, or receive coverage through policies made available through their employment. For older citizens who were retired and not working, Medicare and Medicaid provided health coverage. This was a bit more than a mere safety net, since Medicare was available for everyone sixty-five and older regardless of wealth or income, but it still retained the possibility of individual choice.

One of President Bill Clinton's first priorities in 1993 was national health care. The task force for drafting the proposal was headed by First Lady Hillary Clinton. One of the Clintons' core principles was that everyone needed to be covered under the proposal in order to control costs. This was to be accomplished by requiring everyone to have health insurance and mandating that every employer provide it. Indeed, the Clinton plan was quite similar to, and a precursor of, Obamacare.[7] It created health care exchanges and limited choices of plans. The notion of constructing a large federal bureaucracy for health care was heavily criticized, as was Hillary Clinton's leadership of the project, and ultimately it became clear that there was not sufficient support in the Congress to enact it.

When national health insurance was pushed through Congress in 2010—on a straight party-line vote with no Republicans supporting it—rugged individualism suffered in two ways. First, federal policy and bureaucracy removed many choices about health insurance coverage from individuals and shifted them to the government. Second, the individual mandate—called the individual shared responsibility payment—removed any element of individual consent and required nearly universal participation. One must ask why those individual freedoms were removed in passing health care reform, and whether it was essential to do so. Otherwise, the approach of Lyndon Johnson and the Great Society, leaving room for both individual policies and a government safety net, would seem to be the balanced approach that would better respect both the rugged individual and the forgotten man.

In the early going, President Obama said that the first restriction on individual freedom—taking away your current policy—would not be a problem, famously promising: "If you like the plan you have, you can keep it. If you like your doctor, you can keep your doctor, too."[8] But fairly soon after adoption, millions of plans were declared "illegal" under Obamacare for not conforming to the law's requirements. It was a myth that you could keep your policy if you liked it, since 6.3 million policies were cancelled for not meeting the ACA's standards in 2013, for example.[9] If you were a single male adult with a policy that met your needs, that was no longer a legal choice under Obamacare if it did not include maternity services. Lower rates for healthier people were no longer available since insurance companies could no longer underwrite based on health.[10] So the nature of health insurance policies was prescribed by the government, removing individual choice and the availability of policies tailored to one's own individual needs.

But the bigger blow to rugged individualism from Obamacare was the individual mandate, which requires that people either buy health insurance that complies with the program or pay a tax or penalty. The idea of a federal law requiring that individuals purchase something is a challenge to rugged individualism on its face. As Senator Chuck Grassley concluded, "To my knowledge . . . never in 225 years has the Federal Government said you had to buy anything."[11] Broccoli had its moment of fame when Justice Antonin Scalia, among others, wondered whether, under the same reasoning, the federal government could also "make people buy broccoli." Ultimately, the US Supreme Court held that, although Congress lacked the constitutional power to make people engage in interstate commerce by purchasing something, the federal government nevertheless had the power to impose a tax on people who did not purchase health care.[12]

To better understand the extent of this invasion of personal liberty, one might ask why the individual mandate was included. The claim was that, unless everyone participated, young and healthy as well as old and infirm, the costs could not be controlled and covered. Further, there was concern about the free rider effect in which people who did not buy health insurance nevertheless became a burden on the health care system when they showed up at emergency rooms for free treatment. So the solution was to get everyone to buy in by imposing a penalty or tax if they did not.

It turns out that this was just one of many aspects of the Affordable Care Act that needed a lot more study and debate before enactment because these defenses of the individual mandate are not holding up. In fact, the former chair of the Democratic National Committee, Howard Dean, admitted later that "the individual mandate was not necessary."[13] As health care policy expert Avik Roy pointed out, the free rider problem only accounts for a small part of health care costs, hardly a justification for the individual mandate.[14]

Beyond that, the individual mandate has not worked in accomplishing its goals. Expectations had been that from 20 million to 27 million people would enroll in Obamacare plans by 2016 but, in October 2015, the administration downgraded that target to only 10 million.[15] In a March 2016 report, the Congressional Budget Office increased its estimate of the number left uninsured under Obamacare through 2019 to 27 million, well over its 2010 estimate of 22 million.[16] One contributing problem is that there are far more people with exemptions to Obamacare than expected. The Congressional Budget Office and Joint Committee on Taxation reported that, of the 30 million uninsured in the United States, about 27 million will not be held to the individual mandate because they fall under one of the exemption umbrellas.[17] A related problem is that many of these are younger people, so that the pool of those insured begins to skew older and more expensive to cover.

An additional problem is that people are often finding it cheaper to pay the penalty or tax than to enroll in Obamacare and pay the premiums. In one study in South Florida, for example, a coordinator for enrollment found that about one fourth of those assisted ended up paying the penalty rather than buying health insurance.[18] Economist Douglas Holtz-Eakin, in testimony before the House Ways and Means Subcommittee on Health in April 2015, said that 6.3 million people paid the penalty in 2014, but more than 30 million did not buy health insurance, again in large part because of exemptions. He concluded: "In reality, the individual mandate has been less of a mandate and more of a suggestion." So it would appear that the mandate and associated penalty are not a huge incentive to sign up for health care and that, overall, Obamacare has not made a major dent in the number of uninsured, which was its primary goal.

One can debate the wisdom of Obamacare, and even its accomplishments, especially since it largely federalized "health and welfare" which had formerly belonged to the states, created a huge federal bureaucracy, has had limited success in bringing the uninsured into the fold, and has continued to see costs rise dramatically. But the question we raise here is whether it was necessary to adopt a single mandatory federal program, as opposed to allowing individuals to keep their own policies and doctors. The Obamacare experience seems to suggest that declaring a national crisis and rolling in with a single federalized solution is of limited effectiveness while, at the same time, undermining individual freedom and choice. With the federal government following a similar approach—declaring a war on something and then federalizing it—on poverty, drugs, illiteracy, education, and health care, it is surely time to wake up and realize that leaving room for individuals and states to make their own choices and do their own work makes a good deal of sense. If rugged individualism is no longer the American system, it at least deserves a seat at the table, which it did not receive under Obamacare.

But despite being signed into law in 2010, as of 2016 Obamacare is still not settled. There are continuing votes to repeal it, and the Republican candidates for president all said they would replace it. There are still court challenges, which have plagued the law from the beginning. And polls suggest that the popularity of the bill has declined over time. This is a sign of rugged individualism, fighting a rearguard battle, over this intrusion into individual lives and decision-making. As Senator Ron Johnson of Wisconsin said, Obamacare is "the greatest assault on freedom in our lifetime."

Education: No Federalizing Left Behind

Perhaps no matter has been considered more classically a state and local concern than K-12 education. Nevertheless, beginning in the 1990s, the locus of power over education, using the lever of funding for education reform, has steadily shifted to Washington, D.C. Federal concern arose in the 1950s when the Russians launched Sputnik and beat America into space, leaving many to worry that our education system, especially science education, needed a major boost. In 1979, President Jimmy Carter brought the federal government more deeply into the field when he established the federal Department of Education. As we have seen before, if you build it, it will regulate. Another milestone along the road to federal concern about education came in 1983 when President Reagan's National Commission on Excellence warned that America's schools faced "a rising tide of mediocrity that threatens our future as a Nation and a people."

But things really began to change when President George W. Bush, who had led new efforts in educational testing and accountability in Texas as governor, decided to tackle education reform from Washington, D.C., as former Arkansas governor Bill Clinton had also done when he became president.[19] Bush joined with Senator Ted Kennedy to pass the No Child Left Behind Act of 2001 (NCLB). While not actually federalizing education, NCLB certainly made the federal government a major player in education policy, requiring cash-strapped states and school districts to establish standards, create annual assessments (tests), and announce results if they wished to qualify for federal NCLB funding. All students (no child left behind) were supposed to be performing proficiently at grade level by 2014. Of course, all of this came at a cost to educational individualism as teachers felt pressure to teach to the test, to ignore subjects not tested and more creative projects, and to focus on bringing up the bottom students more than challenging those at the top.

By 2012, however, it was clear that 80 percent of America's schools would not meet NCLB's proficiency goals in another two years. So Secretary of Education Arne Duncan did the obvious: lower the standards. He began issuing waivers (to over forty states) lifting the law's requirements, but this was only done if the states agreed to new conditions he sought to impose that would further change the direction of K-12 education, including strong moves toward a national curriculum (Common Core) and teacher evaluation and accountability. So if federal regulation does not work, the answer is to waive the regulations but then impose more federal standards. The Obama administration offered Race to the Top grants to schools and states that followed their educational goals, again increasing the federal role in education and a race to uniformity.

By 2015, there had been such a backlash against No Child Left Behind, and also the Common Core curriculum, that Congress realized it could not reauthorize the law without significant changes. In December 2015, following extensive negotiations, Congress enacted the Every Student Succeeds Act to replace NCLB. The new legislation sought to construct a more careful balance between states' rights in education and a federal role. It allows states to develop their own systems, although federal testing will continue. A final compromise allows the federal government to step in when schools are truly failing. But in general, the new law shifts the balance away from the heavy federal role established by NCLB back toward the states. Still, the federal government holds the purse strings for a lot of education money, and it has demonstrated a willingness to use that as leverage to force states and schools to do its bidding. Only time will tell how much might change as a result of the new act.

Education policy, then, through sixteen years and two presidents, has been a story of increasing federalization, regulation, and standardization. The freedom of parents, students, and even teachers to chart out an educational course and pursue it has become more and more limited. Federal testing and accountability have been the dominant education policy theme for nearly twenty years, with very mixed results. Rugged individualism is always at risk in the face of government regulation and standardization, especially at the federal level. Rugged individualism has pushed back, with the rise of home schooling, charter schools and vouchers, and opposition to the Common Core curriculum. But by the time rugged individuals recognize the system has gone too far toward federalization and organize to oppose it, the pendulum has already swung strongly toward Washington and it is difficult to return to the status quo.

Thomas Piketty on Income Inequality and Its Effect on Rugged Individualism

President Obama, in a major address on December 4, 2013, referred to a "dangerous and growing inequality and lack of upward mobility" as "the defining challenge of our time."[20] A few months after this presidential pronouncement, then little-known French economist Thomas Piketty published his now-famous *Capital in the Twenty-First Century*. This monumental work, with its fortuitous timing, has become a seminal book not only in economics but in public policy more broadly, turning Piketty into a bit of a rock star.

The central economic problem of inequality is caused, according to Piketty, when the annual rate of return on capital (r) is greater than the rate of overall economic growth (g).[21] So when wealthy investors are able to earn more—sometimes far more—than recent modest rates of economic growth (1–2 percent), the rich are accumulating wealth at much higher rates than everyone else and income inequality grows. Exacerbating the problem, says Piketty, is the fact that "[d]uring the 1980s English speaking countries reduced the top marginal income tax rate,"[22] weakening a key defense against income inequality. Indeed, he says that the countries "with the largest decreases in their top tax rates are also the countries where the top earners' share of national income has increased the most."[23] Meanwhile, especially in the United States, there were "high remunerations at the summit of the wage hierarchy, particularly among top managers at large firms."[24] All of this has mixed into a heady brew of capital growth for the wealthiest 1 percent of the population, while the rest of the country lags behind.

Whereas World War I, World War II, and the New Deal kept income inequality at bay for much of the twentieth century, Piketty argues that, since the 1980s, inequality has exploded. World Wars I and II forestalled income inequality by building up wages and employment on one hand and wiping out capital accumulations on the other. Public policy also helped limit income inequality through the progressive income tax and the estate tax that limited wealth accumulation. In Piketty's view, the Great Depression killed laissez-faire economics and with it rugged individualism. But in the later twentieth century, according to Piketty's narrative, Margaret Thatcher in Britain and Ronald Reagan in the United States revived individual freedom, and with it income inequality, by dramatically cutting progressive income tax rates and through deregulation and privatization of the economy. This has resulted in the disappearing middle class and the huge inequality problem we now face.

Piketty the economist then enters broader territory to declare that income inequality is a social problem that demands a government solution: much higher tax rates that facilitate the redistribution of wealth. Clearly preferring Jean-Jacques Rousseau and the French Revolution over John Locke and the American Revolution, Piketty quotes favorably in his introduction from the 1789 French *Declaration of the Rights of Man and the Citizen*: "Social distinctions can be based only on common utility."[25] In fact, the normative premise of his book is that high degrees of income or wealth inequality are bad for society and need to be corrected. Piketty follows John Rawls's *Theory of Justice*: "Social and economic inequalities . . . are just only if they result in compensating benefits for everyone, and in particular for the least advantaged members of society."[26] Besides the injustice of income inequality, Piketty argues that "the top centile is a large enough group to exert a significant influence on both the social landscape and the political and economic order."[27] So Piketty finds in income inequality a range of economic, social, and political problems.

In terms of solutions, Piketty rejects the notion that there are self-correcting mechanisms for income inequality, especially since "history and logic show" that an expected economic growth rate of 3–4 percent is "illusory."[28] Pointing out that "there is no historical example of a country at the world technological frontier whose growth in per capita output exceeded 1.5 percent over a lengthy period of time,"[29] Piketty argues that 1–2 percent growth rates are, in effect, the new normal for the United States (and other developed nations), so that we cannot grow ourselves out of this problem. Education cannot explain the large growth in wealth at the top, nor can the market—"the invisible hand does not exist," he says—control it.[30] But in Piketty's view, the only viable solution to the problem is "worldwide confiscatory [tax] rates on top incomes."[31] This would include a tax on capital, which Piketty calls "a new idea designed explicitly for the globalized patrimonial capitalism of the twenty-first century."[32] These heavy taxes must also incorporate a progressive inheritance tax since there is now a patrimonial middle class that owns between a fourth and a third of total wealth.[33] All of this is to enforce "social norms of fair remuneration."[34]

Unfortunately, much of the debate about Piketty's thesis has been limited to economics when, in fact, his larger argument is social and political. Rather than help individuals at the bottom with safety nets, education, and increased productivity, his solution is to tax those at the top, in part to fund social programs, but primarily to make wealth more fairly and equally distributed. His postmodern redistribution theory would consider moving the present level of 50 percent of "public financing" to "two-thirds to three-quarters of national income" by increasing the progressive income tax and revisiting a progressive inheritance tax.[35] What would government do with all this increased revenue? Why stop with government-provided retirement, education, and health care, he asks; why not also include "culture, housing, and travel?"[36] His proposal, in the spirit of the French Revolution, is that America needs to be less concerned about liberty and more dedicated to equality, with a resulting increase in social harmony. "Rethinking the twentieth-century fiscal and social model and adapting it to today's world will not be enough," Piketty concludes.[37] What is needed is a social revolution, prompted by his economic analysis and carried out by government.

If carried out, this certainly seems to be a death sentence for American rugged individualism. Entrepreneurs would lose much of their financial incentive to take risks and make heavy investments in the future. Unless his prescription were followed worldwide, one can easily imagine the Steve Jobses, Bill Gateses, and other business pioneers simply starting their global companies in other countries. The core ownership of private property, long a linchpin of individual liberty, would be undercut by confiscatory taxes on passing along one's property to future generations. To another central question of the ages—what should government do?—Piketty answers "essentially everything." Ironically, this is not because he concludes that government could do it better, or that having government make decisions instead of individuals is more satisfying, but because it is fairer for government to have the money and spend it. All of this is not even "to finance the social state but to regulate capitalism."[38]

Instead of lower-cost experiments, Piketty is ready to bet the farm on radical government solutions to the income inequality problem. Don't we first need a debate on how important income inequality is in our society, as compared with, for example, income mobility? Having recently dropped from larger economic growth rates to more modest 1–2 percent growth, should we not experiment with ways to return to more robust growth before we accept that as the new normal? Should we not discuss ways of improving the lot of individuals at the bottom of the ladder—education, productivity, welfare—before revolutionizing the American system? Are we prepared to say that it is now the role of the government to have over 50 percent of national income to spend, rather than leaving those decisions in the hands of individuals?

Piketty's approach is essentially a kind of soft Marxism. It is Marxist in the sense that the accumulation and distribution of capital is the story, and capitalism, in its natural working, produces inequality, so it requires government regulation. It is soft in the sense that the problem can be solved short of revolution—we can regulate capitalism, Piketty believes. "What kind of social state is most suitable for the age?" he boldly asks.[39] Most assuredly, rugged individualism is not his answer. Indeed, we cannot allow voluntary consent because some force will be required to secure equality. Thus we need strong government to require that people will behave in accordance with the vital principle of equality.

Piketty is the latest version of the 1960s radical economic critique, which in turn dates back to the 1930s, arguing that neither economic growth nor a welfare state is an adequate solution. Instead, radical redistribution is required. Could such a Piketty revolution take place? He acknowledges it could only be done by "collective deliberation."[40] Surprisingly, he leaves room for the decisions not to be made by his economic formulas, but acknowledges that "only democratic deliberation can decide."[41] But he is quite clear that the market will not correct the problem because, in the final analysis, the market is the problem. And so, apparently, is individualism.

Rugged Individualism and the "Zinnification" of American History

Stanford University education professor Sam Wineburg has said that Howard Zinn's *A People's History of the United States* "has arguably had a greater influence on how Americans understand their past than any other single book."[42] The text has sold over two million copies and has been widely used in both high school and college courses. Zinn's approach to American history has been both praised and criticized. As governor of Indiana, Mitch Daniels sought to keep the book out of the hands of students. As Wineburg noted, the book was once considered radical but is now "mainstream" and in some circles "the dominant narrative."[43] In order to appreciate Zinn's impact on our national self-understanding, especially as it pertains to rugged individualism, his interpretation of key events and figures in American history must be reviewed.

Zinn's version of American history begins by undermining the rugged individualism of explorer Christopher Columbus. Rather than seeing Columbus as a discoverer and pioneer, Zinn casts him as a greedy murderer whose message to the native Indians in America was "Show me the gold." So Columbus's discovery of the New World, according to Zinn, is not about the birth of a new frontier, with a hope of equal opportunity, but rather a narrative about the injury and destruction of indigenous peoples. America's founding, which, importantly, Zinn dates to 1492, was therefore based on a kind of original sin by Columbus and his men.

For many historians, 1776, with the American Revolution and Declaration of Independence, and 1787–1789, with the development of the Constitution, were the formative periods for America. When and how one finds the birth of America, and the influences attending it, are critical for the American individualism narrative. Zinn's story suggests America was ill-founded and that "executioners" such as Columbus were hardly the sort of rugged individuals to be admired or emulated. Indeed, Zinn asserts that he is writing a history that is not "on the side of the executioners" but on behalf of the executed or marginalized.[44]

Zinn's history is largely one of resistance and civic action taken by the oppressed. The founding story of 1776 was made up by the upper class and sold to the common man. The Declaration of Independence, according to Zinn, brought this myth to its "peak of eloquence."[45] His concern is with "some Americans [who] were clearly omitted from this circle of united interest drawn by the Declaration of Independence: Indians, black slaves, women."[46] Zinn endorses Charles Beard's economic interpretation of the Constitution, noting that four groups were not represented in the Constitutional Convention: "slaves, indentured servants, women, men without property."[47] The Constitution's checks and balances served no more noble purpose than maintaining order on behalf of the rich few over the many who were poor.

Moving to another central narrative of rugged individualism, the American frontier, Zinn notes that "the Americans assumed now that the Indian land was theirs."[48] His notion of a frontier thesis was how white people imposed their values on the land belonging to others. There were no heroes of rugged individualism out conquering the land or extending the American frontier. What traditional American history recites as "up by their bootstraps" stories of American individualism in the late nineteenth century, Zinn characterizes as a myth: "The Horatio Alger stories of 'rags to riches' were true for a few men, but mostly a myth, and a useful myth for control."[49] And so, to the readers of Zinn's American history, a nation born in the original sin of taking land and killing natives must keep conquering inferior people. Jingoism is the reality and American individualism is a myth.

Zinn's counter-narrative continues into the twentieth century, lifting up the Industrial Workers of the World and activists, artists, and intellectuals such as Eugene Debs, Jack London, and Mary "Mother" Jones. He notes with favor that such thinkers extended the "ideas of Karl Marx . . . that people might cooperatively use the treasures of the earth to make life better for everyone, not just a few."[50] Zinn dismissed the reforms of the Progressives, calling them "a reluctant reform, aimed at quieting popular uprisings, not making fundamental changes."[51] Even the New Deal, according to Zinn, did not fundamentally change the system, as "capitalism remained intact."[52]

One can easily imagine how the last one hundred years of American history have gone, by Zinn's account. World War II was about "advancing the imperial interests of the United States."[53] During the postwar period, even under the more liberal President John F. Kennedy, "the distribution of wealth was still unequal," with laissez faire—let things be—the motto. Zinn reserves some appreciation for the dissenters, not the reformers, such as the 1960s radicals or Betty Friedan's "feminine mystique." Zinn wraps it all up in this comprehensive punch line: "In the sixties and seventies . . . there was a general revolt against oppressive, artificial, unquestioned ways of living. It touched every aspect of personal life."[54] The last fifty years, for Zinn, were "a capitalistic encouragement of enormous fortunes alongside desperate poverty, a nationalistic acceptance of war and preparations for war."[55] Zinn was incensed by Reagan's tax cuts and the "economic illness" they encouraged.[56] The Cold War caused panic among America's leadership, fearing it would now be more difficult to "maintain its military establishment."[57]

Zinn's *People's History*, by its own description, "is a history disrespectful of government and respectful of people's movements of resistance."[58] The

American system, "the most ingenious system of control in world his-tory,"[59] is meant to advance the interest of the rich and powerful against blacks, women, and working-class people.[60] And when it really comes down to it, Zinn takes "the liberty" of uniting all those not in the top 1 percent economically as "the people."[61] Indeed, by the end, Zinn calls for a massive protest movement that would "come together in the next century, the next millennium, to fulfill the promise of the Declaration of Indepen-dence, of equal rights to life, liberty, and the pursuit of happiness."[62]

Zinn also undermines American rugged individualism. For one thing, he joins the Progressives in reducing this broader religious, philosophical, and political idea into a purely economic one. Individualism, to Zinn, only works for the Spanish, or the landowners, or the upper 1 percent. The rags-to-riches American dream, in Zinn's world, is only a myth, and a dangerous one at that. The American constitutional system was not created so that interest would counteract interest and thereby protect individual liberty, but rather to keep Zinn's "people" under control and unable to attain power and wealth. The United States is not about Herbert Hoover's American individ-ualism with equality of opportunity because, for the 99 percent, there is no opportunity.

In a powerful way, the counter-narratives of Howard Zinn and Thomas Piketty connect with each other and with the Progressives of the early twentieth century. The only understanding of American history and poli-tics that is truly valid is an economic one, and that story is about the wealthiest 1 percent guarding its wealth and power from the rest of the people. It is a cynical narrative indeed, undermining any hope for Ameri-can rugged individuals to conquer new frontiers and achieve any kind of hopeful destiny.

The Constitution and Rugged Individualism

Among academics and policy thinkers, a narrative has developed that America's nearly 230-year-old Constitution is antiquated and in need of an extreme makeover. In a sense, this is nothing new—Charles Beard's *An Economic Interpretation of the Constitution of the United States* in 1913 set the pace for a good deal of today's debate. The liberal critique is that the Constitution's many checks and balances, which may have made more sense in an earlier and simpler time, are now thwarting the federal government from stepping up to the many challenges of our society today. Since American rugged individualism is embedded in and protected by the founders' intricate framework of constitutional balances of power and checks and balances, this new fix-the-Constitution narrative tends more toward a big-government, collectivist agenda than one that would protect American individualism.

As we argued in chapter 1, the Constitution was designed to protect individual rights, both through explicit declarations of rights (such as the Bill of Rights) and through institutional checks and balances to limit the power of government against individuals. The academic critique primarily takes on the latter, arguing that these checks and balances construct unfortunate and inappropriate barriers to action by the federal government and, worse, are undemocratic. Instead, many contemporary constitutionalists argue we need a kind of parliamentary system, with fewer checks and balances, so that the party in power, elected by the people, can get more done without gridlock and obstruction.

To illustrate, consider four important books by constitutional scholars over the last decade and the sorts of recommendations they propose. In 2008, constitutional law professor Sanford Levinson published *Our Undemocratic Constitution*. Levinson's premise is "that I have become ever more despondent about many structural provisions of the Constitution that place almost insurmountable barriers in the way of any acceptable notion of democracy."[63] Levinson argues that, as a result of a number of "wrong turns" taken at the founding, we "must recognize that substantial responsibility for the defects of our policy lies in the Constitution itself."[64] His bottom line is that the Constitution is insufficiently democratic, and he proposes a number of structural fixes to make it more so. Structures such as federalism and separation of powers are, in his view, blocking the democratically desirable majority rule. But the Constitution was not intended to govern a pure democracy, but rather a democratic republic. Various checks and balances were intended to protect individual rights and make certain that the "cool and deliberate sense of the community,"[65] and not the passions of a faction in the moment, would prevail.

A year earlier, in 2007, Professor Larry Sabato published *A More Perfect Constitution*. The subtitle of the book reveals its purpose more fully: *23 Proposals to Revitalize Our Constitution and Make America a Fairer Country*. Sabato's core argument is that America's "historic progress" toward fairness and equity "is being eroded and impeded by archaic parts of the original United States Constitution."[66] Since the Congress, for example, is no longer sufficiently representative of the people, we should grow the size of both the Senate and the House and, while we're at it, impose term limits. We should strengthen the presidency but reduce it to one term, with the possibility of a two-year performance bonus. We should reform the Electoral College, put term limits on judges, and so on. In short, Sabato argues that America's political systems are antiquated and need to be brought up to date, all to be accomplished at a convention of the states to propose constitutional amendments. All this hearkens back to Woodrow Wilson's "science of administration" as the heart of the matter—if we could just fix the systems, everything should work fine, or at least much better.

Constitutional law professor Louis Michael Seidman wrote *On Constitutional Disobedience*.[67] His short version in the *New York Times* was appropriately titled "Let's Give Up on the Constitution."[68] In it, Seidman argues that the real culprit behind our broken system of government is "our insistence on obedience to the Constitution, with all its archaic, idiosyncratic and downright evil provisions." Imagine, he says, that Congress and the president want to take a certain course of action for the good of the country, but feel inhibited by the fact that "a group of white propertied men who have been dead for two centuries, knew nothing of our present situation, acted illegally under existing law and thought it was fine to own slaves might have disagreed with this course of action." Instead, Seidman says it's time for constitutional disobedience, staying with the broad strokes of the document but coloring outside the particular lines where necessary to get things done.

Most recently, a more conservative Hoover Institution scholar, Terry Moe, joined the attack on the "antiquated" constitution. In a book co-authored with William G. Howell, he argues that the Constitution does not allow for government to be "effective."[69] After attacking the usual suspects—checks and balances, separations of power—Howell and Moe argue that Congress is more beholden to the localized concerns of its constituents than to solving the national problems we face. Their solution is to increase the power of the president. Another Hoover scholar, Richard Epstein, disagrees, pointing out that the founders' allocations of power make more sense than increasing the role of the already powerful executive branch.[70] Howell and Moe seem tied to the notion that government must "do something," in spite of the fact that the federal government's solutions—Obamacare, Dodd-Frank—seem worse than doing nothing. We would argue that gridlock, though not ideal, is better than bad policy. And, if anything, the power of the legislative branch, which most closely represents the people, needs to be strengthened vis-à-vis the executive and judicial branches, not weakened.

Just as it is difficult to love an ugly founding, it's hard to love an ugly Constitution. And an ugly, antiquated, obstructionist Constitution is precisely the portrait these scholars are painting. But note carefully how their notions of a more perfect, a more beautiful Constitution are rooted. They are starting from the perspective that the Constitution is supposed to be about democracy with a fully flowered guarantee of equity and equality. But the founders were suspicious of pure democracy and were clearly drafting a Constitution to support something quite different: "a republic if you can keep it," as Benjamin Franklin famously said. Yes, the US Senate is not fully democratic, allowing two senators for every state regardless of size, but in the balance of power established by the founders, it serves the important purpose of federalism. The Electoral College, always a popular target, is not strictly democratic, but it gives both the states and the people a role in electing a president. These separations of power and checks and balances are no accident—indeed, they serve their purpose of protecting individuals in a democratic republic. The scholars, however, argue that, in this day and age, democracy should enable the good of the whole which can only be decided by a strong and unrestrained federal government.

The current liberal ire toward the Supreme Court and its application of the Constitution was galvanized by *Bush v. Gore* in 2000, the case in which the Supreme Court was accused of taking the election away from the popular vote winner, Al Gore, and giving sufficient electoral votes to George W. Bush to win the presidency. To critics of the Constitution and the Court, this was an infuriating example of using an antiquated and undemocratic constitutional mechanism, the Electoral College, and conservative judicial activism to steal the election from the democratically elected candidate. As a consequence, unable to muster the support needed to amend the Constitution to do away with the electoral system and move to a direct democratic vote for president, critics instead sponsored the National Popular Vote Bill, which, when enacted by states with sufficient electoral votes to choose a president, will require those states to cast their electoral votes for the winner of the national popular vote. This is a slick end-run around the Constitution that has been introduced in every state and, as of this writing, has already passed in eleven states with 165 electoral votes.

But historically one must turn the calendar back even further to understand the present constitutional debates and their effect on individualism. *Brown v. Board of Education* in 1954 launched the modern constitutional era, demonstrating the willingness of the Supreme Court to entrench itself deeply into questions of public policy, in this case school segregation, and to expand the reach of the Fourteenth Amendment and its guarantee of "equal protection." Part of the Reagan Revolution of the 1980s was an emphasis on reining in the Court and appointing more conservative judges. The history of the last thirty years, especially, has been one of pitched political battles over Supreme Court nominees and bitter disappointments when this or that judge lets his or her side down. In addition to *Bush v. Gore*, liberals have recently been angry about *Citizens United v. Federal Election Commission* (2010), in which the Court chose freedom of speech over equality of speech, with the Left viewing this as re-empowering the robber barons (their understanding of rugged individualism) on the political scene. It is shades of Charles Beard and his economic argument against "the myth of rugged individualism."

Even as Progressive constitutional scholars today would undo some of the Constitutional processes that protect rugged individualism, so too would courts and judges weaken the protection of individual rights guaranteed in the Constitution. The phrase "equal protection" under the Fourteenth Amendment is rapidly becoming a kind of super-text in the Constitution, able to strike down or limit freedoms guaranteed in other places. Take the First Amendment, for example. The "free exercise of religion" is now limited in speech ("happy holidays") and practice (do not violate the "equal dignity" of gay marriage). The Second Amendment right to bear arms is under attack, even though some of the worst gun violence has been committed in states such as California that have the toughest gun control laws.

Worst of all, the Tenth Amendment, guaranteeing that powers not given to the federal government are reserved to the states and individuals, is in steady decline in the face of the need of the federal government to provide "equal protection" to every citizen. Health care is in crisis, so we adopt an omnibus federal law to take over the states' prior responsibilities for health and welfare. So that "no child [is] left behind," we allow the federal government to take over the state and local governments' traditional role in overseeing K-12 education.

Where, then, are the champions of individual rights in the Constitution? It is difficult to find many. There are a precious few in the academy, on the bench, and in the Congress. The forces of constitutional interpretation and understanding blow left, not right; they blow collective and not individual; and they blow "equal protection" and not "freedom from." In the end, the primary constitutional protection for individualism may turn out to be the difficulty of amending the Constitution, requiring two-thirds of each house of Congress and three-fourths of the state legislatures to do so, under Article V. Nevertheless, there is a movement to accelerate constitutional change by bringing together a convention of the states under Article V.

Conclusion

In the modern era, it seems as though American rugged individualism is hanging on in the face of heavy winds. Tocqueville's warning that Americans would prefer equality over liberty seems to be playing out. While the heavy winds of the income inequality debate blow against free markets, the winds of social equality threaten individual freedom. The Constitution, both in court and in the scholarly realm, is pressed to give up some of its checks and balances and restraints on government in favor of democracy, while the Fourteenth Amendment's "equal protection" clause looms ever larger. The federal government has taken up a pattern of declaring war on our domestic problems and fashioning federal solutions, leaving little room at the table for individual (or even state) solutions.

Yet no final revolution has come. The rugged individual still survives and fights back. Obamacare is not settled. Income inequality is still a debate. The Supreme Court issues some decisions that restrict federal overreach. The rugged individual has been weakened by modernity but not destroyed. He lives to work and play another day.

Notes

1. Barack Obama, "Remarks by the President on the Economy in Osawatomie, Kansas," December 6, 2011, https://www.whitehouse.gov/the-press-office /2011/12/06/remarks-president-economy-osawatomie-kansas.

2. David Davenport, "Rugged Individualism Is Exactly the Wrong Case for Obamacare," *Forbes*, June 15, 2015, http://www.forbes.com/sites/daviddavenport/2015/06/15/rugged-individualism-is-exactly-the-wrong-case-for-obamacare/#3e51b8fd17a8.

3. David Davenport, "Cory Booker and the Democrats Distort History for Political Purposes," *Forbes*, July 27, 2016, http://www.forbes.com/sites/daviddavenport/2016/07/27/cory-booker-and-the-democrats-distort-history-for-political-purposes/#5b06f8787ef2.

4. Thomas Sowell, *Intellectuals and Society* (New York: Basic Books, 2009), 282, 284.

5. Howard Zinn, *A People's History of the United States: 1492–Present* (New York: Harper Perennial Modern Classics, 2005).

6. Thomas Piketty, *Capital in the Twenty-First Century* (Cambridge, MA: Harvard University Press, 2014).

7. For the history of Clinton's health care approach and its impact on Obamacare, see Scott Gottlieb, "The Clintonian Roots of Obamacare," *National Affairs*, no. 24 (Summer 2015).

8. Barack Obama, "Weekly Address: President Obama Outlines Goals for Health Care Reform," June 5, 2009, https://www.whitehouse.gov/the-press-office/weekly-address-president-obama-outlines-goals-health-care-reform (and on many other occasions as well).

9. Tim Phillips, "Obamacare Cancellations, Again," *USA Today*, October 16, 2014, http://www.usatoday.com/story/opinion/2014/10/16/obama-health-care-insurance-cancellation-column/17353673/.

10. See David Hogberg, "20 Ways Obamacare Will Take Away Our Freedoms," *Investors Business Daily*, March 22, 2010.

11. Statement of Senator Chuck Grassley of Iowa to the Senate, on November 30, 2009, Cong. Rec., 111th Cong., 1st sess., 2009, vol. 155, no. 175, S12005.

12. *National Federation of Independent Business v. Sebelius*, 567 US, 132 S. Ct. 2566, 183 L. Ed. 2d 450 (2012).

13. David Sherfinski, "Howard Dean: Individual Mandate in Obamacare Wasn't Necessary," *Washington Times*, December 30, 2013, http://www.washingtontimes.com/blog/inside-politics/2013/dec/30/dean-individual-mandate-wasnt-necessary/#!.

14. Avik Roy, "Myths of the 'Free Rider' Health Care Problem," *Forbes*, February 2, 2011, http://www.forbes.com/sites/theapothecary/2011/02/02/myths-of-the-free-rider-health-care-problem/#4c30c7e1689a.

15. Paige Winfield Cunningham, "Administration expects little progress on Obamacare enrollment," *Washington Examiner*, October 15, 2015, http://www.washingtonexaminer.com/administration-expects-little-progress-on-obamacare-enrollment/article/2574233.

16. Congressional Budget Office, "Updated Budget Projections: 2016–2026," March 24, 2016, https://www.cbo.gov/publication/51384.

17. See, e.g., John Merline, "87% of Uninsured Can Avoid ObamaCare Mandate Tax: CBO," *Investor's Business Daily*, June 5, 2014, http://www.investors.com/politics/obamacare/obamacare-individual-mandate-loophole-cbo-finds/.

18. Chabeli Herrera, "When Paying the Obamacare Penalty Is Cheaper Than Buying Insurance," *Miami Herald*, May 15, 2015, http://www.miamiherald.com/news/local/community/miami-dade/article21105861.html.

19. As a precursor to federalization of education reform, literacy policy was federalized in a similar way. See David Davenport and Jeffrey M. Jones, "The Politics of Literacy," *Policy Review* (April/May 2005): 45–57.

20. Barack Obama, "Remarks by the President on Economic Mobility," December 4, 2013, https://www.whitehouse.gov/the-press-office/2013/12/04/remarks-president-economic-mobility.

21. Piketty, *Capital in the Twenty-First Century*, 260.

22. Ibid., 333.

23. Ibid., 509.

24. Ibid., 298.

25. Ibid., 1.

26. Ibid., note 21, 631.

27. Ibid., 254.

28. Ibid., 93–94.

29. Ibid., 93.

30. Ibid., 315, 332.

31. Ibid., 512.

32. Ibid., 532.

33. Ibid., 376–77.

34. Ibid., 333.

35. Ibid., 483.

36. Ibid., 480.

37. Ibid., 515.

38. Ibid., 518.

39. Ibid., 471.

40. See, e.g., ibid., 513.

41. Ibid., 562.

42. Sam Wineburg, "Undue Certainty: Where Howard Zinn's *A People's History* Falls Short," *American Educator* (Winter 2012–13): 26–34.

43. Ibid., 27, 32.

44. Zinn, *A People's History*, 10.

45. Ibid., 70.

46. Ibid.

47. Ibid., 91.

48. Ibid., 87.

49. Ibid., 254.

50. Ibid., 339.

51. Ibid., 349.

52. Ibid., 403.

53. Ibid., 411.

54. Ibid., 536.

55. Ibid., 563.

56. Ibid., 580.

57. Ibid., 592.

58. Ibid., 631.

59. Ibid., 632.

60. Ibid., 635.

61. Ibid., 632.

62. Ibid., 682.

63. Sanford Levinson, *Our Undemocratic Constitution: Where the Constitution Goes Wrong (And How We the People Can Correct It)* (New York: Oxford University Press, 2008), 6.

64. Ibid., 9.

65. The *Federalist Papers*, No. 63, http://avalon.law.yale.edu/18th_century /fed63.asp.

66. Larry Sabato, *A More Perfect Constitution: 23 Proposals to Revitalize Our Constitution and Make America a Fairer Country* (New York: Walker, 2007).

67. Louis Michael Seidman, *On Constitutional Disobedience* (New York: Oxford University Press, 2012).

68. Louis Michael Seidman, "Let's Give Up on the Constitution," *New York Times*, December 30, 2012.

69. William G. Howell and Terry M. Moe, *Relic: How Our Constitution Undermines Effective Government—And Why We Need a More Powerful Presidency* (New York: Basic Books, 2016).

70. Richard Epstein, "A More Modern Constitution?" *Defining Ideas*, June 6, 2016, http://www.hoover.org/research/more-modern-constitution.

CHAPTER FIVE

RUGGED INDIVIDUALISM: THE WAY FORWARD

T HE FAMOUS PHILOSOPHER Yogi Berra said, "It's tough to make predictions, especially about the future." In order to predict the future of rugged individualism in America, it should help to recount briefly what we have learned it is and is not. President Obama, no great fan of rugged individualism, has acknowledged that it is nevertheless "in America's DNA" and that it "defines America." Reaching back to the founding, rugged individualism has defined American character and uniqueness. It has been described as the "master assumption" of American political and economic thought. The combination of individual liberty in America's founding and the frontier spirit provided the rich soil in which it has grown and developed.

Equally, it seems important to note what American rugged individualism is not. It is not, as Tocqueville acknowledged, the selfish, isolating self-absorption of the French *individualisme*, since Americans temper their individualism with other qualities such as pragmatism and a disposition toward forming voluntary associations. It is not a purely economic idea, as the Progressives and New Dealers suggested, since it is grounded in a political philosophy of individual rights of many kinds. As Herbert Hoover, who coined the phrase "rugged individualism," pointed out, it is not a laissez-faire, devil-take-the-hindmost philosophy for the wealthy since, in America, it is accompanied by equality of opportunity. It is not, as it is sometimes perceived to be, some form of selfishness or greed that demands it be regulated, presumably by government.

In order to evaluate the future of rugged individualism, it is also useful to review the environments in which it has fared well and those that have hampered and undermined it. In general, rugged individualism is closely tied to frontiers, not just frontiers of the Old West but economic, social, and political frontiers. Where there are new frontiers to conquer, Americans are more likely to launch out in a spirit of rugged individualism. Further, those political climates that tend to favor individual liberty have been most hospitable to rugged individualism. To put it another way, when the American tension that Tocqueville observed between equality and liberty tends toward liberty, rugged individualism has prospered. When the political climate has shifted more toward equality, it has not. Indeed, one could well argue that, since the rise of Progressivism and the New Deal in the early twentieth century, rugged individualism has been under rather steady attack and has often fought even to maintain a seat at the public policy table.

In order to undertake a balanced assessment of the future prospects for American rugged individualism, we should consider reasons to be pessimistic as well as reasons to be optimistic about it. Such an evaluation might also indicate where supporters of rugged individualism might focus greater encouragement and resources, and where it seems important to stand and fight.

Reasons to Be Pessimistic

The political climate in the United States provides plenty of reasons to be pessimistic about the future of rugged individualism. In the 2016 presidential campaign, on the one hand it may have seemed encouraging that rugged individuals such as Donald Trump and Bernie Sanders—who seem not to care much about their party, the establishment, or the present political system—enjoyed surprising success. On the other hand, one could equally be discouraged that voters were apparently less interested in being rugged individuals themselves as they were in supporting rugged, or even somewhat ragged, individuals for the presidency. In other words, Americans seem content to let the government do more and more for them, yet they are intrigued by contrarian individuals such as Sanders and Trump as their leaders.

Despite their unusual personas, neither Sanders nor Trump demonstrated much commitment to individual rights or moving America toward greater rugged individualism. Sanders openly described himself as a democratic socialist interested in an expanded welfare state. His campaign planks included greater government regulation and single-payer health insurance, with free college and pre-K education for everyone. Sanders has been deeply concerned about income inequality, prepared to enact significant tax increases in order to fund his expensive programs. His agenda was clearly more soft collectivism and less rugged individualism.

Donald Trump's political philosophy has been more difficult to ascertain. Perhaps it is best described as nationalism or nativism: make America great again; build physical walls along the borders and tariff walls around the economy. But it is more difficult to see how his philosophy would play out within the borders of the United States as it pertains to collectivism versus individualism and regulation versus individual freedom. Looking for clues, he is certainly in favor of gun rights under the Second Amendment. But his statements about limiting Muslims and their rights raised questions about his understanding of the religion clauses of the First Amendment. His idea of free speech and a free press under the First Amendment has been that he gets to say what he wants, but he would like to open up the libel laws against the media. His broad understanding of presidential power was not especially hopeful for states' rights under the Tenth Amendment. You did not hear him talk much about liberty or freedom. In short, it would seem that Trump's nationalism and promised use of executive power generally is unlikely to rally a spirit or a political and legal climate that favors rugged individualism.

Hillary Clinton represents the mainstream Democratic position, which, though less extreme than Sanders's, travels down that same Progressive road. She wants the government to achieve more collectivist goals, such as wider access to pre-K through college education, but is less certain that it could be entirely free. She sought wider access to health care but did not openly advocate single-payer health care as Sanders did. Clinton originally favored raising the federal minimum wage to $12 per hour, while Sanders supported $15 per hour (and Clinton eventually agreed). You get the point. Whereas Sanders is a full-throated Progressive, or self-described democratic socialist, Clinton represents Progressivism-lite: a third less calories than your full-on Progressive. Still, Clinton is all about the federal government doing and guaranteeing more, with individualism more of a problem than part of any solution. The rise of the administrative state, which removes the crucial element of individual consent, should be a continuing cause for concern regarding the future of rugged individualism.

With Trump as the Republican nominee, the traditional conservative wing of the party wasn't even represented in presidential politics this year, which is itself a disappointment to proponents of rugged individualism. Nevertheless, it has been difficult in recent years to find consistent support for rugged individualism even among conservatives. The largest federal encroachment on K-12 education, the No Child Left Behind law, was enacted with bipartisan support and signed by self-proclaimed "compassionate conservative" President George W. Bush. Likewise, Bush supported a major and expensive expansion of prescription benefits for the aged. Although a few conservatives in Congress have fought the good fight, the federal budget, executive power, and federal regulation all seem to grow under both Republicans and Democrats. All that to say: if you were looking for a stirring renaissance of rugged individualism, you probably would not look in Washington, D.C., or among the leading national politicians or political parties.

Another reason to be pessimistic about rugged individualism is that its foundation, individual liberty, has increasingly become an abstraction in our modern society. Young people, in particular, have grown up in an era of big government and don't entirely understand or appreciate the case for less government involvement in individuals' lives. When those in our society have needs, people have trouble understanding conservatives' preference to have churches and nonprofits take the lead, rather than government. Occasionally there are "liberty moments," when people scratch their heads and wonder why government is invading their personal lives. The attempt to ban large sodas in New York was one such example, although the New York Court of Appeals ultimately ruled that such a law exceeded the city's regulatory authority. Many young people who expected to keep their own private health insurance policies faced an unpleasant surprise when those policies were declared illegal because they did not meet Obamacare requirements. Young men were left to wonder why they had to buy more expensive policies that included pregnancy coverage, for example, which they did not need. Still, overall, such moments are rare and do not seem to meld into much of a liberty movement, especially among the young.

Developmentally, several trends would lead to pessimism about the future of rugged individualism. Helicopter parents, who closely track their childrens' lives at all ages and who intervene with their teachers, bosses, and other authorities, create a climate where rugged individualism becomes a difficult path to pursue. A college experience that now polices "trigger words" and "microaggressions," while adopting policies to keep students from experiencing discomfort, leads more toward coddling than rugged individualism. Then the rising number of college graduates who live with their parents, are older when they find full-time employment, and who marry later all contribute to a generation that will be delayed or prevented from reaching the sort of individualism experienced by their post–World War II parents and grandparents.

Finally, narratives are gaining a hold on the young that will lead America further away from rugged individualism. Robert Putnam argues in his recent book, *Our Kids: The American Dream in Crisis,* that income inequality is the big problem in our democracy today, one that precludes "our kids" from realizing the American dream of upward mobility.[1] One might praise efforts to address income inequality as enlightened commitments to help those lower on the economic ladder; yet each step in that direction mandated by government does necessarily reduce individualism. It places government squarely in the business of income redistribution, something previously the province of individuals. In fact, some polling has suggested that American young people are now more open to socialism than before. A YouGov survey in January 2016 showed that among those under thirty, socialism rated ahead of capitalism, 43 percent to 23 percent. A Reason-Rupe survey in 2014 found 58 percent in favor of socialism for those aged eighteen to twenty-four. All this is tempered, however, by evidence that young people do not even know what socialism means.[2]

Reasons to Be Optimistic

On the other hand, people have been proclaiming the demise of rugged individualism for more than one hundred years, yet somehow it lives on. Planted deeply in the soil of the American founding and character, it may be diminished but is not likely to be destroyed. The more interesting question is whether it might enjoy some kind of renaissance in the twenty-first century. Are there reasons to be optimistic about the future of rugged individualism, or will the future simply see further decline?

If, as we have argued, American individualism is especially nourished in a frontier environment, might today's young people live on some new frontiers where individualism could be nourished? The answer would appear to be "yes." In the information age, young people will live on new social and business frontiers that could very well produce a revival of individualism.

The social media world in which Americans, especially younger Americans, now live is truly a new frontier. Now, rather than leaving the house to engage the collective culture, we are able to be alone and yet through technology also be connected to others. We may not be bowling alone, as Robert Putnam bemoaned, but people are communicating alone. In fact, a new term describes this frontier: networked individualism. Books such as *Networked: The New Social Operating System*[3] and websites such as the Pew Internet Project[4] describe in detail how people are able to operate with greater individualism, yet not in isolation. New and larger social networks are developed, new work styles are possible, new hobbies and interests are pursued—all from the stance of an individual and a piece of technology. As Lee Rainie and Barry Wellman concluded in *Networked*: "The *networked operating system* gives people new ways to solve problems and meet social needs. It offers more freedom to individuals . . . because now they have more room to maneuver and more capacity to act on their own."[5]

It is difficult to evaluate at this early stage the impact of networked individualism on our society and politics, and whether it represents a new boost of energy for American rugged individualism. Whether social media has a positive or negative effect on social relationships is debated, with some agreement that it may extend the range of social contacts and keep some aging relationships alive, while perhaps reducing the depth of relationships.[6] In any event, there is no question that the rise of technology has led to increases in people's alone-time and use of social media, which certainly creates the possibility for a new generation much more inclined toward individualism, or at least networked individualism. As the authors of *Networked* concluded: "The internet allowed users to be both more networked and be more assertive as individuals."[7]

Similarly on the business front, young people seem to be gravitating away from careers in large corporations and toward startups, portfolio jobs, and the "gig economy." Some of this has been driven by the economic downturn starting in 2008, but it is a matter of preference as well. A survey of the college graduating class of 2015 by the consulting firm Accenture revealed that only 15 percent preferred to work for a large corporation.[8]

Professor Tomas Chamorro-Premuzic of University College London confirms this, saying, "In the 15 years I've been teaching MBA students, their career plans have changed dramatically. Until the early 2000s they aspired to work in traditional corporate jobs. . . . In the past few years, however, a new favorite career choice has emerged—working for themselves or launching their own business."[9] As millennials make up a growing percentage of the workforce, this will be a powerful trend in the coming decades. Valuing personal freedom over money and prestige, young people's business lives may increasingly represent a kind of rugged individualism along with their social lives. Starting their own businesses, or stitching together a series of portfolio or gig jobs, will certainly put more "rugged" back into the business lives of young people.

Individualism in business leads to greater creativity and innovation, to be sure. A 2005 study by two Cornell University professors considered collectivism and individualism in group settings, for example, finding that individualistic groups were more creative and generated more innovative ideas.[10] It makes sense, then, to think of companies like Uber or Lyft, which have transformed entire fields of business and customer service, as the new John Waynes of the rugged individualism economy.

It is unclear how these changes in business and social life might translate into the larger society and politics, or how they might affect the philosophy of rugged individualism. On one hand, young people spending more time in their business and social lives in an individual role would point toward more individualism, broadly speaking. On the other hand, it is not clear that younger voters see the connection between their own increasingly individual lifestyles and supporting rugged individualism, as opposed to collectivism, in the political realm. In general, the younger generation has been less interested in politics and more engaged in volunteer or community activities. But when they do vote, or jump onto the political bandwagon, they readily support more collectivist and liberal causes, such as Bernie Sanders's free tuition or nationalized health care. So while changes toward individualism in their work and social lives seem to offer the possibility of greater interest in rugged individualism, so far the connection between individualism in one's personal life and a political philosophy is not apparent. Still, it seems worthwhile for proponents of rugged individualism to educate young people along these lines.

There is also hope for rugged individualism in the lives and businesses of immigrants who still flock to the United States. Immigrants continue to come to America, seeking a better life and more opportunity for themselves and their children. When you take a taxi ride in a major US city, your driver is frequently an immigrant who, if given the chance, will tell you how he is working hard so that his children will enjoy the American dream. It is immigrants who study up on American history and civics in order to pass the citizenship test, a commitment that few born here undertake with comparable results. As Milton Friedman pointed out, however, even the rugged individualism of immigrants is threatened by the growing American welfare state and the emphasis on ethnic identity. Friedman noted that his wife, Rose, was herself an immigrant, and he was a child of immigrants, but warned that the pro-American spirit of their generation would be threatened in the future "as the melting pot has increasingly been replaced by multiculturalism, and rugged individualism by a welfare state."[11]

Another reason to be optimistic about the future of rugged individualism is that people keep dragging their feet against many of the government's efforts in collectivist planning. In Los Angeles, for example, drivers have resisted the ideas of urban planners and the additions of carpool lanes and mass transit because of their individual preferences to hop in the car and drive.[12] As former Los Angeles County Transportation Commission member Wendell Cox points out, while government planners have pressed hard for rapid transit, the user numbers have declined, costs have gone up, and traffic has increased. He concludes that "drivers have not shifted to transit, despite billions in federal transit funding."[13]

Other examples of public resistance to collectivist ideas at the federal level include opposition to Obamacare and Common Core. Even though Obamacare was enacted in 2010, public opposition to it remains high at nearly 50 percent,[14] and lawsuits continue to be brought on account of its overreach. It is quite remarkable that this major federal initiative continues to face significant opposition six years after enactment. Common Core was well on its way to approval across the states when people began to recognize it as a significant government encroachment on local authority over school curriculum, at which time it became increasingly unpopular and efforts were undertaken in several states to repeal it.[15] Indeed, Common Core and various social policies applied to schools have caused an increase in home schooling, which is yet another grassroots form of individualism resisting collectivism. Remarkably, home schooling has grown over 60 percent during the last decade.[16]

It is wise for rugged individuals to appreciate what has been settled by the deliberate sense of the community over time, and what is still open for debate, discussion, and resistance. Some things are settled: Social Security will not be taken away, unless it runs out of money, for example. But Obamacare is not settled—it is still challenged in court and repealed in the House of Representatives (though not in the Senate) and unpopular in the polls. So just a vote, especially a party-line vote, doesn't necessarily settle things. It turns out that No Child Left Behind wasn't settled—it was challenged so often and so strongly, especially by teachers, that it was not reauthorized. Gun control, the role of God in the public square, and many other issues are not settled and are worthy of debate and resistance.

Finally, we should note continuing interest by many Americans in our nation's founding. People still flock to Mount Vernon, Monticello, the National Archives, and Philadelphia to learn about the founders and the founding. And quite amazingly, the hottest and most awarded musical on Broadway, *Hamilton*, explicitly celebrates the story of one of America's founders, Alexander Hamilton. Born of a mixed-race mother in the West Indies, Hamilton came to America as an immigrant; the cast that celebrates his life and contributions is primarily black and Latino, encouraging all kinds of Americans to identify with the story. And despite efforts to remove Hamilton from the $20 bill, following a hue and cry, he remains.

Hamilton suggests there is untapped interest in the complexities of the founding, which could be encouraged by more creative civic education.

Strengthening What Remains

A New Testament scripture, Revelation 3:2, written to a lukewarm church in Sardis, seems apt: "Wake up, strengthen what remains and is about to die." A reawakening to the value of American rugged individualism is timely, along with efforts to strengthen its resources and increase its opportunities for influence. At the same time, it may also be important to play a little defense against those forces that seem to have rugged individualism constantly in their crosshairs and under assault. At the very least, the goal should be to maintain rugged individualism as an appropriate element of American character that should be valued and kept at the table of public life.

Certainly America needs to wake up to the value and importance of rugged individualism properly understood. The sheer passage of time from the founding and the pioneering frontier days allows Americans to fall asleep and forget some of their core values. And for some, the idea of rugged individualism is so attached to the frontier heroes that it is difficult to carry it forward to a time when, arguably, the country has evolved to become less independent and more interdependent. To some, rugged individualism sounds like an anachronism from a much earlier time. And then we must admit that rugged individualism has had real enemies who have sought to undo it and replace it. The Progressives, in particular, have fought rugged individualism on at least two grounds. Either they have sought to attach it to the Old West and open frontiers, rendering it irrelevant when the country was settled and people began to live together in cities; or they have shrunk it down to a set of selfish economic motives of the robber barons of yesterday, or the top 1 percent today, and have sought to attack it as unworthy of America.

Americans need to be reawakened to rugged individualism as more than a John Wayne cowboy of the West or a robber baron of the East. It is foremost a starting point of analysis for our unique society. America did not begin with the church or the state or the king as the center of things, but instead the individual. It is the individual who is the unit of analysis in America, and everything else proceeds, as a series of choices, from that starting point. We may choose a government or church or a particular kind of society, but those choices are made by Americans as individuals. We must not fall asleep on that core dimension of rugged individualism.

We must also be reawakened to the centrality of individual liberty, or individual rights, that are at the core of rugged individualism. The Declaration of Independence declares those individual rights, and the Constitution, especially the Bill of Rights, protects them. Such rights are not anachronisms from another time, but are active and vital today. As Herbert Hoover warned when he returned to the United States from war-torn Europe, we must never give up our unique freedoms to the various totalitarianisms that were sweeping the Continent. We must be ever alert to the danger that government stands ready to limit our individual freedoms in favor of some other good—be it government takeovers of education or health care, or diminution of our freedoms of religion or speech, or allowing individual liberty to become a mere abstraction. We must be reawakened to these cornerstones of rugged individualism in each generation. As Jefferson said, the world belongs to the living, and each generation must work out its own understanding of things. We should neither have a blind veneration for the past (*Federalist* No. 14) nor deprive the past of its due veneration, without which government could not maintain its stability (*Federalist* No. 49).

One approach would be to identify and label "liberty moments," especially for the younger generation, times when their frustration with government should be more deeply understood as a challenge to their individual liberty. As mentioned earlier, efforts to regulate the size of soda beverages was one such moment when people recognized that the government was going too far. But the real problem was the invasion of individual liberty—after all, who should be deciding what size beverage cup people buy? Surely not the government. Another such missed opportunity came when the government declared millions of individual health insurance policies to be illegal because they did not contain all the protections government thought should be there. It turns out that many of those missing provisions had nothing to do with the health of the individual purchasing the policy—maternity care for young men, for example—but were one more super-sized government regulation to try to make the economics of federalized health care work. Once again, this was a liberty moment and, in addition to denouncing the misleading government promise that if you liked your health care you should keep it, critics should have gone deeper to identify the attack on individual liberty. These efforts could help make individual liberty less of an abstraction and more of a priority for a younger generation so accustomed to big government.

Then, in the words of the Scripture, we must strengthen and protect what remains. The founders thought that the several checks and balances and separations of power in the Constitution were important to protect individual rights, especially against the passions of the moment and the power of government. So rugged individualism, even today, relies on that very constitutional system for protection. Calls to break down the federalism structure—whether by strengthening executive power, or turning to some kind of parliamentary system, or allowing the courts to take over our social and economic decisions—are a kind of declaration of war against individual rights. They are packaged more seductively, of course, as evolutionary steps in the development of a complex republic or as ways of breaking down barriers to government action. But now, as then, we need our federalist structure to protect American individualism. On every issue we should continue to ask a vital set of questions: Is this something the government should do? If so, which branch: executive, legislative, or judicial? And which level: federal, state, or local? These are the protections our constitutional system affords to individualism and liberty.

Here's another idea: when we ask the first question, whether an action is appropriately one for government or not, we should restore individual action as the default answer. In other words, the individual should again be the starting point of analysis, not the government. Instead, the government often falls into the trap that it must do something, even if the action it takes is not likely to solve, and sometimes doesn't even address, the real problem. As one example, governments lined up to ban hand-held phones in cars, even though there was evidence that the real problem was not the physical distraction of holding a phone, but the driver inattention caused by talking on the phone.[17] Government reaction to the economic crisis, despite evidence that government policy frequently worsens the economy, is a larger example.[18] In the case of Obamacare, there were policy options that would have helped the uninsured that did not inhibit the liberty of individuals to buy their own policies. The economic argument—that the funding only worked if everyone was in it together—has certainly not played out to be accurate, with a huge uninsured population despite massive investment in a misguided program. In an effort to do something, government often ends up doing the wrong thing. We must halt this notion that government is responsible for everything and must, in every case, do something.

The nation's schools of public policy and government are also part of the difficulty. Basically their idea of teaching public policy is to identify a problem and then sort through possible government solutions, ignoring the fact that "public" policy is much broader than just government.[19] Putting the public back into public policy would mean exploring what individuals, nonprofits, communities, businesses, and other nongovernmental entities might do, as well as government action. And even within the realm of government solutions, these schools focus primarily on national and international solutions to problems, not local approaches that may be more effective. In effect, schools of public policy are institutionalizing the mistaken approach of Woodrow Wilson, Franklin Roosevelt, and other Progressives that if only we had the right national experts or enlightened administrators able to run the federal system, things would be better, despite considerable evidence to the contrary.[20]

Improving civic education in America would also strengthen the spirit of rugged individualism. The most recent NAEP (National Assessment of Educational Progress) test results from spring 2015 showed that only 18 percent of eighth-grade students were "proficient" or better in history and only 23 percent in civics or government.[21] Polls consistently show that young people cannot name one of their home state US senators, nor do they understand basic elements of the Constitution. Without an understanding of the American system—or worse, with a kind of distaste for American history from misguided high school textbooks—young Americans will be hard-pressed to champion constitutional governance or protect individual rights. With federal funding for civic education eliminated in 2011, and only resumed in 2016, and with the major emphasis on science, technology, engineering, and math (STEM), civic education has taken a back seat. Civic engagement has become a battle cry in education, which is fine—but it needs to be preceded by civic education. The states need to get busy requiring courses in civic education, and schools of education should make sure their graduates understand enough of the content of the American system to teach it effectively. Ronald Reagan, in his farewell address, called attention to the need for an "informed patriotism" in which we teach our children "what America is and what she represents in the long history of the world."[22] Making certain that people are able to provide informed consent as citizens is very much a part of strengthening rugged individualism.

Finally, we need to be open to new formulations and partnerships for rugged individualism. As Tocqueville pointed out, American individualism was never a purely selfish, inwardly focused kind of individualism. Americans combined their individualism with a volunteer spirit, a tendency toward forming associations, and other practical qualities. Hoover, who coined the term rugged individualism, said that in America it was always combined with equality of opportunity. President Obama, a critic of rugged individualism, nevertheless acknowledges its place in the American character, adding that it has always been "bound by a set of shared values" and by "a sense that we are in this together." The key is that Americans begin with individualism and then consent to various associations, beginning with the family and reaching out into the larger world.

So what new associations or qualities might make rugged individualism stronger and more a part of American life without losing its essential character? For young people, especially, rugged individualism combined with a strong sense of community may seem attractive. Their experience of "networked individualism" through technology is one example of this. Their commitment to community service and civic engagement reinforces this modern combination. Even the pioneers of the West often banded together to help one another build houses and communities, so this notion of rugged individualism combined with community could increasingly become what American individualism looks like.

And what of the word "rugged"? Should it continue to be part of the formula? Dictionaries use words like "toughness," "determination," "durability," and "strength" to define "rugged." Are Americans still rugged today? Do we need to be? Recent books suggest that it is still an important part of American character and success. *The End of Average* tells author Todd Rose's story of going from food stamps to head of a center at Harvard University and his discovery that so much in America is based on average needs, when in fact no one is average.[23] Similarly, *Grit: The Power of Passion and Perseverance* makes the case for how individual determination makes the real difference in today's world.[24]

It could be that the term "rugged" needs a bit of updating. Might "resourceful" be a term that carries a similar sense, with a more modern outlook? Indeed, young people today will need to be resourceful to have the kind of future that they want. In a rapidly changing world, with difficult economic and national security challenges, resourcefulness, even ruggedness, will be needed to survive and prosper. When Herbert Hoover first used the expression in 1928, he sought to contrast American rugged individualism with the soft despotism and "paternalism" of Europe, which has been closing off its frontiers with a fixed hierarchy and settled order for a few hundred years now. One would hope that there would at least be room for this understanding in the ongoing description of American character.

Can Government Change with New Frontiers?

Our book does not primarily concern the psychology or sociology of individualism, but rather how government policy affects rugged individualism. So, we close by examining the role of government vis-à-vis the new signs and frontiers of individualism. Back to our core questions about federalism (is an issue a matter for government at all, and if so, which branch and which level?), we are seeing government consolidation in an era of individual and societal fragmentation. The federal government is taking over more and more matters and is consolidating its power, especially executive power, at a time when nearly everything else in society—business, social life—is returning to smaller, more individualized and localized approaches. This continuing growth of the administrative state is a special concern to rugged individualism because it removes the crucial element of consent.

One way to describe the problem is to say that the federal government is still, after eighty years, building on the paradigm of the New Deal. Federal consolidation that took place in the midst of the Great Depression is still the way government operates today. It is as though the federal government thinks it's still the 1930s or the Great Society of the 1960s, but it's clearly not. The federal government taking over K-12 education and health care is the wrong direction to go. Continuing to build out a federal welfare state, as Bernie Sanders and even Hillary Clinton propose, is a misguided effort to ramp up the federal system of an earlier time. Even expanded welfare states such as Denmark are learning that, in the worldwide economic downturn, government cannot afford to continue everything it has been doing, much less add more.[25]

A classic example of the problem created by the old systems is the pension crisis now confronting state and local governments. In a day when government jobs did not pay as well as those in the private sector, governments offered attractive retirement pensions as an extra incentive. Now, however, many government staff positions pay as well as any job, and while the private sector has moved to defined contribution plans, government still has those attractive guaranteed pensions. Now the bill on these unrealistic policies has come due, with recent estimates showing over $1 trillion in unfunded public pension benefits.[26] These deficits, caused by unrealistic investment and coverage policies, have already bankrupted some governments and are threatening many others. The generosity of the administrative state, living off borrowed money and not facing new realities as the private sector has done, turns out to be costly indeed.

Professor Jay Ogilvy, noting eroding confidence in large institutions, argues that "day by day, week by week, year by year we are experiencing a gradual but pervasive spread of individual autonomy and increasing confidence in personal judgment."[27] While acknowledging the dangers of too much[28] individualism, Ogilvy notes the collectivism of Russia and Japan, concluding that "the dangers of excessive individualism are nothing compared to the oppressiveness of excessive collectivism." Decentralization and splintering are occurring around the world, Ogilvy argues, creating more individualism and therefore greater opportunity to address geopolitical problems in new ways. Indeed, isn't the common good best discovered and pursued through a bottom-up, rather than a top-down, process that leads to conversation and consent?

One approach to addressing excessive federalization is proposed by Yuval Levin in his recent book *The Fractured Republic*.[29] Levin argues that what is needed is neither excessive federal regulation from above, nor too much selfish individualism from below, but instead increased attention to the several community-based and localized actors in the middle such as family, work, and religious communities.[30] In responding to the new frontiers of twenty-first-century life, Levin rightly concludes that "political power needs to be dispersed just as other forms of power have been."[31] Neither the Left nor the Right has the best approach, he says, though the

Right may be closer because of its basic view in favor of decentralization.[32] The assumption is that leadership from these sectors closer to the level of the individual is more likely to be effective than continuing to grow the federal behemoth in Washington.

Columnist and think tank member Jonah Goldberg would look for new institutions in the political arena. He reminds us of the American Liberty League of the 1930s, "a legitimate grass-roots educational and political organization with more than 100,000 members."[33] In a situation not unlike 2016, the League was "a platform for constitutionalists and classical liberals who felt estranged from political parties."[34] In a time when candidates such as Trump and Sanders embrace nationalism and socialism respectively, perhaps it is timely for a political movement that is more centrist and that believes in ideas, not just winning.

We live in a time of economic, business, and social transformation in which Americans are more concerned about security than usual. Some of the anger and frustration are about globalization and technology reducing lower-paying jobs. The appropriate role for government in such a situation is greater emphasis on education and retraining for new higher-paying jobs, including tax policies better targeted at this. But along with security, people are also interested in the American dream. Candidates like Bernie Sanders don't want the American dream, they want to transform it to the Danish dream. Too much emphasis on safety and security actually threatens the American dream. The core message of the Left—we'll give you food stamps so you won't starve, health care so you don't suffer from a disease, and social security and welfare so you have money—is so much about security and protecting the downsides of life that it leaves little room for the upsides, which are available through individual liberty.

To keep the American dream vital and alive, we will need rugged and resourceful American individualism. We cannot continue to build a stifling federal government and an overwhelming national debt and leave room for rugged individualism. We cannot tip the delicate balance between equality and liberty so heavily in favor of equality that there is no liberty left for individual Americans to enjoy and employ. The new frontiers of the twenty-first century call us to rekindle the rugged individualism of America's founding, frontiers, and Constitution. It deserves a continuing, vibrant role in American politics and life.

Notes

1. Robert Putnam, *Our Kids: The American Dream in Crisis* (New York: Simon & Schuster, 2015).

2. David Davenport, "America's Drift toward 'Socialism' Is Generational, but Also Educational," *Forbes*, February 26, 2016, http://www.forbes.com/sites /daviddavenport/2016/02/26/americas-drift-toward-socialism-is-generational -but-also-educational/#76e84d3171ed.

3. Lee Rainie and Barry Wellman, *Networked: The New Social Operating System* (Cambridge, MA: MIT Press, 2012).

4. Pew Internet Project, http://www.pewinternet.org.

5. Rainie and Wellman, *Networked*.

6. R. I. M. Dunbar, "Do Online Social Media Cut through the Constraints That Limit the Size of Offline Social Networks?" *Royal Society Open Science*, January 20, 2016, http://dx.doi.org/10.1098/rsos.150292.

7. Rainie and Wellman, *Networked*, note 5, 70.

8. Jeanne Sahadi, "Where Do Millennials Want to Work? Not at Corporations," *CNN Money*, May 12, 2015, http://money.cnn.com/2015/05/12/pf /millennials-work/.

9. Tomas Chamorro-Premuzic, "Why Millennials Want to Work for Themselves," *Fast Company*, August 13, 2014, http://www.fastcompany.com/3034268 /the-future-of-work/why-millennials-want-to-work-for-themselves.

10. Jack Goncalo and Barry Staw, "Individualism-Collectivism and Group Creativity," *Cornell University ILR School*, November 1, 2005, http://digitalcom mons.ilr.cornell.edu/obpubs/1/.

11. Milton Friedman and Rose D. Friedman, *Two Lucky People: Memoirs* (Chicago: University of Chicago Press, 1998), p.x.

12. Fred Siegel, "Traffic Talk," *City Journal*, Spring 2016, http://www.city -journal.org/html/traffic-talk-14345.html.

13. Wendell Cox, "America Needs a Rational Transit Policy," Heritage Issue Brief 4368 on Transportation, March 24, 2015, http://www.heritage.org/research/reports/2015/03/america-needs-a-rational-transit-policy.

14. Real Clear Politics, "Public Approval of Health Care Law," http://www.realclearpolitics.com/epolls/other/obama_and_democrats_health _care_plan-1130.html.

15. Morgan Polikoff, "What Drives Common Core Opposition?" May 31, 2016, http://c-sail.org/common-core-opposition.

16. Susan Berry, "Number of Homeschooled Children Soars in America: Up 61.8% Over 10 Years," May 19, 2015, http://www.breitbart.com/big-government/2015/05/19/number-of-homeschooled-children-soars-in-america-up-61-8-over-10-years/.

17. David Davenport and James Prieger, "Cell-Phone Bill Based on Faith, Not Research," *San Francisco Chronicle*, September 14, 2006, http://www.sfgate.com/opinion/article/Cell-phone-bill-based-on-faith-not-research-2487819.php.

18. Scott Sumner, "Making Things Worse—Government Must Do Something So Why Not the Wrong Thing?" June 3, 2016, https://incentiveseverywhere.com/2016/06/03/making-things-worse-government-must-do-something-so-why-not-the-wrong-thing/.

19. See Pete Peterson, "Trump, Sanders and the Populist Anti-Policy Surge," *Wall Street Journal*, May 19, 2016.

20. See James Piereson and Naomi Schaefer Riley, "The Problem with Public Policy Schools," *Washington Post*, December 6, 2013.

21. David Davenport, "Hamilton Is a Hit on Broadway, But Not in the Classroom," *Forbes*, January 29, 2016, http://www.forbes.com/sites/daviddavenport/2016/01/29/hamilton-a-hit-on-broadway-but-not-in-the-classroom/#642c392a22a1.

22. Ronald Reagan, "Transcript of Reagan's Farewell Address to American People," *New York Times*, January 12, 1989, http://www.nytimes.com/1989/01/12/news/transcript-of-reagan-s-farewell-address-to-american-people.html?pagewanted=all.

23. Todd Rose, *The End of Average: How We Succeed in a World That Values Sameness* (New York: HarperCollins, 2016).

24. Angela Duckworth, *Grit: The Power of Passion and Perseverance* (New York: Scribner, 2016).

25. David Davenport, "Bernie and Hillary Beware: Something Is Rotting in Denmark," *Forbes*, November 1, 2015, http://www.forbes.com/sites/daviddaven port/2015/11/01/bernie-and-hillary-beware-something-is-rotting-in -denmark/#25f42c725fbd.

26. Joshua D. Rauh, "The Public Pension Crisis," *Defining Ideas*, April 12, 2016, http://www.hoover.org/research/public-pension-crisis.

27. Jay Ogilvy, "The Global Spread of Individualism," *Stratfor Global Intelligence*, October 14, 2015, https://www.stratfor.com/weekly/global-spread -individualism.

28. Ibid.

29. Yuval Levin, *The Fractured Republic: Renewing America's Social Contract in the Age of Individualism* (New York: Basic Books, 2016).

30. Ibid., 8, 203–5.

31. Ibid., 196.

32. Ibid., 141.

33. Jonah Goldberg, "With Constitutionalists Feeling Abandoned by Both Parties, It's Time to Bring Back the Liberty League," *Los Angeles Times*, May 31, 2016, http://www.latimes.com/opinion/op-ed/la-oe-goldberg-liberty-league-201 60531-snap-story.html.

34. Ibid.

ABOUT THE AUTHORS

David Davenport is a research fellow at the Hoover Institution at Stanford University, where he has also served as counselor to the director and director of Washington, D.C., programs. He previously served as president of Pepperdine University, where he was also a professor of law and public policy. He is a regular columnist for Forbes.com and has previously been a columnist for the *San Francisco Chronicle* and Scripps Howard News Service. He is also a contributing editor to Townhall.com and delivers regular radio commentaries on the Salem Radio Network. He and Gordon Lloyd co-authored *The New Deal and Modern American Conservatism: A Defining Rivalry*. He has contributed chapters to Hoover Press books, articles for *Policy Review*, *Defining Ideas*, and the *Hoover Digest*, and is co-author of the book *Shepherd Leadership*.

Gordon Lloyd is a senior fellow at the Ashbrook Center and the Dockson Professor Emeritus of Public Policy at Pepperdine University. He is co-author of three books on the American founding and is editor of James Madison's *Debates in the Federal Convention of 1787*. He is the co-author, with David Davenport, of *The New Deal and Modern American Conservatism: A Defining Rivalry* and author-collaborator on three books on political economy. He is also the creator of four websites on the creation and ratification of the Constitution and the Bill of Rights. He also serves on the National Advisory Council for the Walter and Leonore Annenberg Presidential Learning Center through the Ronald Reagan Presidential Foundation.

INDEX